America's current standoff with North Korea, is dangerous, complex, and replete with poor options for resolution. The United States is in a high-stakes game of chicken with the rogue nation that will have significant consequences no matter which path is chosen by each side.

Should war break out in North Korea, the scope would be beyond any war to date. Millions, perhaps tens of millions of people would die. All North Koreans are taught from a young age that America is evil and will attack the North. Citizens are told it is their duty to fight to the death to save their country. It should be anticipated that many will do just that. Anyone over 17 has had military experience, since all North Koreans are required to serve in the military for 3 years.

While American's think the entire world is against North Korea and that all countries abide by UN sanctions, this is not entirely true. The North's allies are often the same countries that present challenges to the United States, such as Iran, Syria, Cuba, Yemen, and Somalia. North Korea circumvents sanctions through barter exchanges of goods and technology.

North Korea has vast bunker networks which can shield large portions of its population. They can wait out an American attack and then counter-attack when the opportunity is best.

Missiles and nuclear weapons allow the possibility that any war may reach the American mainland as well. Civilians in the U.S. are soft and often unaware of or unaffected by ongoing U.S. military engagements. There is a significant threat that there will be attacks upon U.S.

1

territories and that civilians will die, even if the missile and nuclear threats can be neutralized.

Even if North Korea lost its ability to strike the U.S. mainland, it could choose secondary targets belonging to American allies in Japan and South Korea, or American troops in the region.

Although North Korean terror attacks were mainly constrained to the 1970s and 1980s, terrorism is still a weapon in the North's arsenal. Given that the North has chemical and biological weapons, such an attack could be devastating.

There is little doubt that if America does not act, the technology currently available to North Korea will increase in sophistication. There is also little doubt that this technology will be sold to others for profit. Failure to act would leave the world far less safe than it is today.

If America does act, it must commit to a long and horrific war. The U.S. will, of course, win any war with the North but the costs in terms of world opinion, military, and financial loss will be staggering. There is also a high risk that any war has the potential of expanding to China and Russia, both of which border North Korea. The North has strategically placed its nuclear and missile programs close to these borders.

For the moment, both sides are caught in an unwinnable game of chicken. This book will help explain the current quagmire, challenges hindering diplomacy, and possible alternatives to all-out war.

Life in North Korea

North Korea is one of the most mysterious and reclusive countries on earth due largely to the its political and social isolation from most of the world. Much of America's knowledge about life inside North Korea comes from defectors, spies, and people who risk their lives to get information out of the hermit nation.

Tourism does exist in North Korea, but it is limited. Those who visit North Korea are usually restricted to the capital city of Pyongyang. Pyongyang is a city that is restricted to North Koreans who are the most loyal to the regime. Only government officials and those tied to the government have access to private vehicles. Tourists may not travel alone. They have limited, if any, contact with the local population and what they are allowed to see is highly controlled and orchestrated.

(Pyongyang)

In North Korea, citizens need a certificate issued by the government to travel from place to place. Only those

3

who are deemed to be the most loyal to the regime are permitted to reside in or visit the capital of Pyongyang. This policy provides the regime with an additional layer of protection from its own citizens. Aside from Pyongyang this policy is especially guarded for people allowed to live near and work in Kaesong because there is a lot of exchange going on there with South Korea. Kaesong is a special industrial zone on the border of South Korea. As part of the "sunshine" outreach of 2002, South Korea collaborated with the North to provide around 50,000 factory jobs to North Koreans. This collaborative effort allowed a much-needed influx of cash to the North. North Korean citizens who are authorized to work in this zone are chosen for their demonstrated loyalty to the North's regime. Even those people who are most trusted by the government, work under heavy scrutiny. Any lapse in judgment or unsanctioned communication about life in the North can result in the workers and his or her entire family being severely punished, including parents and children. The pressure to remain loyal is great.

(Kaesong Special Industrial Zone)

In North Korea there is no freedom of speech or freedom of the press. Criticism of the regime or the leadership in North Korea, if reported, is enough to make a citizen and his or her family 'disappear' from society and end up in a political prison camp or facing execution. There is no free media inside the country. The only opinion allowed to be voiced inside the country is that of the regime. The media of North Korea is amongst the most strictly controlled in the world.

The government controls all radio and television stations. Radios and televisions in North Korea are pre-tuned to North Korean stations and must be checked and registered with the police. Some North Koreans own Chinese radios which can receive foreign stations but listening to foreign broadcasts is prohibited and the punishment is severe. Foreign broadcasts are jammed and due to planned incompatibility between television systems in the North and South, South Korean television programs cannot be received in the north. There is an active black market for the sale of USB flash drives containing foreign entertainment, despite the threat of severe punishment.

Elite citizens have limited access to government approved foreign news sources. China has trained several North Korean journalists to covertly report events inside North Korea. Journalists have risked their lives to provide footage of executions to foreign media.

In North Korea there is no freedom of information. Propaganda is far reaching beginning in primary school where children are taught that the United States is evil and American soldiers kill and eat Korean children. Children, like all the population, are told that the Kim family are living Gods. Control of information extends to art which often depicts the victories of North Korea, the God-like nature of the Kim family and the evil of America.

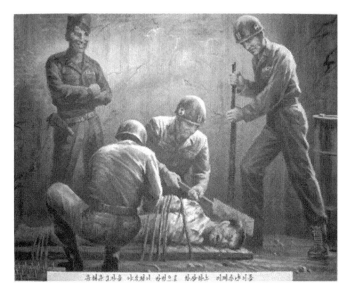

(Americans Portrayed as Torturers in North Korean Art)

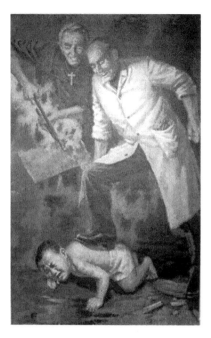

(American Doctors and Clergy Depicted Torturing Baby)

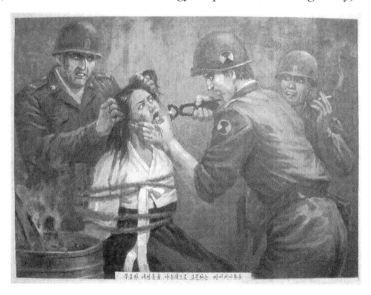

(American Soldiers Depicted Torturing Woman)

(American Soldiers Depicted Nailing Document to Woman's Head)

Knowing the threat that outside information poses to their propaganda and ideology, and the governments control over the people, the regime has invested massive resources in trying to maintain an information blockade and keep its monopoly as the only source of information and ideas available to the North Korean people. It is illegal to own a tunable radio in North Korea, there is no access to the Internet (except for a few hand-picked and monitored officials), and North Korean landlines and mobile phones cannot make international calls.

North Koreans are forced into leadership adulation. The regime forces the people to participate in the maintenance of personality cults around the Kim leaders that have ruled the country for over 60 years. Propaganda starts in nursery school and a large proportion of the curriculum for all students, even at the university level, is dedicated to memorizing the official yet mythical history of the Kim family. State media provides a constant stream of myths about the Kim's and lauds the sacrifices they supposedly make for the people. The public are taught that the Kim's are Gods, and because they are Gods, amongst other things, they do not urinate of defecate. Millions of labor-hours that could be used to develop the economy have to be spent idolizing the leaders instead.

There is no religious freedom in North Korea. Organized religion is seen as a potential threat to the regime and therefore nothing apart from token churches built as a facade of religious freedom for foreign visitors are allowed. Thousands of Buddhists and Christians have been purged and persecuted throughout the history of North Korea. People caught practicing or spreading religion in secret are punished extremely harshly, including public executions, or exile in political prison camps.

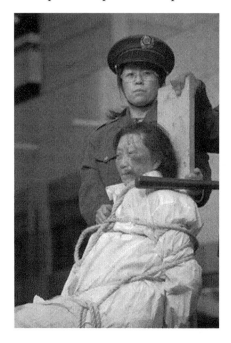

(Photo of Tortured Christian Smuggled Out of North Korea)

Both the North and the South use helium balloons to send propaganda into each other's countries. Private groups in the South often attach USB flash drives with news, entertainment, and messages for people in the North. Being caught with these flash drives in the North can result in severe punishment.

North Korea faces chronic food shortages, especially in the poor rural areas. The majority of food produced or received through aid is consumed by the elite people living in prominent areas such as Pyongyang. Those in rural areas suffer greatly. Grass is a staple part of their diet and when famine hit rural people hard, defectors claims of cannibalism began to be reported through foreign news reports. The official stance of the North Korean government is no food crisis exists and that any hardships faced by the North Korean population are caused by the United States, South Korea, and Japan. Despite the current nuclear stand-off, the United States, South Korea, and Japan still provide humanitarian aid to North Korea. The government's propaganda tells the general population that these food sources have been poisoned by state enemies and should not be consumed. The humanitarian aid meant to help the starving population are hoarded by the elite living in cities such as Pyongyang.

(Malnourished Children in Rural North Korea)

The regime's refusal to reform its failed agricultural policies, combined with adverse climate conditions, and an inability to purchase necessary agricultural or food imports mean that the North Korean people have faced food shortages ever since the 1990s. Millions of malnourished children and babies, pregnant women and nursing mothers suffer most due to the shortages today. This has left an entire generation of North Koreans with stunted growth and a higher susceptibility to health problems.

The regime claims that it provides universal health care to its people. In reality, the majority of the public healthcare system collapsed in the 1990s, with only prioritized hospitals in areas such as Pyongyang kept functioning. Elsewhere, health services and medicine are only available to those that can afford it. Ordinary North Koreans are therefore afflicted by easily preventable or curable poverty-related diseases, such as tuberculosis and cataracts.

The North Korean regime has invested an incredible amount of time and resources creating the songbun system, a form of political apartheid that ascribes you with a level of perceived political loyalty based on your family background. A person's particular songbun level (there are 51 of them) can then restrict their life opportunities, including where they can live, educational opportunities, party membership, military service, occupation, and treatment by the criminal justice system. Any perceived political infractions by a family member will lead to their songbun being demoted.

Historically North Korea has threatened its neighbors as a negotiation tactic to receive more aid. Until now, it posed little threat to its neighbors and appeasement was used as a diplomatic tool to decrease tensions with the North. The North is also well aware that when Libya (voluntarily surrendered), Iraq (facilities destroyed by Israel), and Syria (facilities destroyed by Israel) lost their nuclear development programs, they were invaded. At the same time, Iran's refusal to give up its nuclear program resulted in an influx of money and the lifting of sanctions.

North Korea may be protecting itself from invasion by flaunting its nuclear capabilities or it may be hoping for a cash windfall like what befell Iran. North Korea is used to bullying its way into receiving concessions from others and may be hedging its bet that, as in the past, aggression will be met with appeasement. President Trump, however, is not a career politician and has spoken out against the appeasement of past U.S. Presidents. He has invested in a show of strength that must have North Korea questioning its redundant strategy. Both sides have a great deal to lose as diplomatic attempts become exhausted.

Officially, political prison camps do not exist in North Korea, but they do. Five political prison camps are known to hold an estimated 80,000 to 120,000 people. Some of them are the size of cities, and they have existed five times as long as the Nazi concentration camps and twice as long as the Soviet Gulags. Many people imprisoned in these camps were not guilty of any crime, but were related to someone who supposedly committed a political crime. Often, those held have no idea what that crime was, and even children who are born in the camps are raised as prisoners because their blood is guilty. Forced labor, brutal beatings, and death are commonplace. The regime denies the existence of these camps, but multiple survivor testimonies have been corroborated by former guards as well as satellite images.

In North Korea, if your relative is persecuted for anti-state or anti-socialist crimes, then you and three generations of your family can be punished for it. The aim is to remove from society the whole family unit to prevent any dissent from emerging in the future, and to deter martyrs who might sacrifice themselves for a political cause but would not want to sacrifice their whole family.

Public executions are used as a warning to the people not to go against the establishment rules. Top military and government officials, elites, and even members of the leaders own family are not immune to execution. The method of execution varies but is usually quite gruesome. Citizens, including school children, are forced to watch. Defectors report executions occurring by people being fed to starving attack dogs, shot with anti-aircraft weapons, being blown apart by jet engines, and quartering.

The North Korean regime publicly executes citizens who have been accused of a variety of crimes, including petty theft. Whole communities are forced to watch these executions, which are designed to instill fear amongst the people and deter them from doing anything that could be seen as against the regime's wishes.

The North Korean regime makes it illegal to leave the country without state permission, but every year thousands of North Koreans risk their lives to escape. If caught trying to escape, or if caught in China and sent back, they are at risk of harsh punishments including brutal beatings, forced labor, forced abortions, torture, and internment in a political prison camp. Those suspected of having had contact with South Koreans or Christians while in China receive the most severe punishments.

North Korean refugees' well-founded fear of persecution if repatriated means that they should be protected under international refugee law. However, the Chinese government prioritizes its political relationship with Pyongyang and does not recognize them as refugees. Instead they label them as "economic migrants" to justify the forcible repatriation of thousands of North Korean refugees every year.

Since coming to power, the Kim Jong-Un leadership has cooperated with the Chinese authorities to tighten border security. Recent defectors have told the outside world of increased physical border security, increased risk associated with bribing border guards, and heightened punishments for people trying to escape. Fewer defectors have made it to China and the number of refugees managing to arrive in South Korea has decreased by almost half.

North Korean refugees in China live in a precarious and desperate situation. They fear harsh punishment or even death if they are caught and sent back to North Korea, but many do not have the resources or contacts to get themselves out of China. Their illegal status forces them to work in invisible industries and leaves them vulnerable to exploitation by unscrupulous employers and sex traffickers, as they have no recourse and no protection from authorities.

Many North Korean women who escape North Korea become victims of sex trafficking. China's lack of marriageable women, especially in the rural areas of its Northeast provinces, creates a demand for North Korean women who are at risk of being forced to work in brothels or are bought and sold as wives. North Korean women have been sold for as little as a few hundred dollars in China.

After the state-socialist economy collapsed in the 1990s, the regime was no longer able to provide for the people, and up to a million North Koreans lost their lives due to famine. Through this great adversity the North Korean people had to survive by their own strength, and engaged in illegal market activities and foraging to get food. This led to a process known as marketization from below.

North Korean women, in particular, emerged from more traditional roles to play a key part of this process, and to this day many market activities continue to be female-dominated. The market became the primary source of food for ordinary North Koreans outside the ruling elite, and as food markets gradually grew to encompass a broader range of goods and services, the market mindset and profit motive spread throughout North Korean society.

Over the past decade the regime has vacillated between grudging tolerance and active crackdowns on the markets, but the people have proven their resilience. After the 2009 currency reform debacle the regime must now realize that the markets are a fact of life that they must learn to live with.

The famine and grassroots marketization triggered unprecedented levels of internal and cross-border movement and trade with the outside world, much of it illegal. The influx of foreign consumer goods, primarily from China, and their spread through North Korea's markets is giving the people tangible evidence of the advancement of their neighboring countries.

Until recent technological advances, the North Korean regime had few things to sell to the outside world apart from natural resources and obsolete weapons. They are desperate for foreign currency. North Korea counterfeited foreign money, including American 100.00

bills. They have also counterfeited products, particularly American cigarettes. They are increasingly selling cheap North Korean labor to foreign countries, and this is exposing growing numbers of North Koreans to the prosperity and advancement of other countries that use more efficient systems of economic governance. The regime takes the majority of these workers' wages, but jobs at foreign companies, whether based in North Korea or abroad, are still keenly sought after by North Koreans.

The Kaesong Industrial Complex (an economic cooperation zone where South Korean companies hire North Korean workers) is helping to spread awareness of South Korea's economic and technological progress throughout North Korean society. North Korean refugees have reported that they heard about the Kaesong Industrial Complex through word of mouth, even though they lived at the opposite end of the country. North Korean workers were known to be paid well to work with South Koreans, producing goods that were far superior to anything produced by North Korean factories.

North Korea, while having limited access to the internet, has an elite group experienced in cyber-crime for government profit. This group has pilfered technology from South Korea and others. It has infiltrated and pilfered electronic banking institutions in other countries and siphoned off Bit-coin transactions.

It now has advanced technological plans for weaponry, missiles and nuclear weapons which could provide North Korea with an abundance of wealth should it decide to share those technologies with other rogue nations.

Under pressure from the United States, China has greatly decreased trade with North Korea. Russia, however, has seized upon China's decreased economic ties to North Korea and increased its own market share of trade with the North.

In North Korea, where the laws are designed to protect an authoritarian regime, there are a lot of potential benefits to ordinary people when the rule of law breaks down. Defectors and refugees report that corruption is rampant and that in North Korea there isn't anything you can't do if you have money.

As the new economic activities are considered illegal, and because many regime officials rely on bribes to survive, corruption is inevitable. Restrictions and crackdowns push more market activity into the illegal/informal sector. Crackdowns have become part political intimidation and part economic predation. Security officials have a high level of discretion in arrest and sentencing. Fear of harsher punishments allow security officials to extract higher bribes, which makes it impossible for the central regime to crack down on private business. Corruption is creating opportunities for those with some money to operate more freely from regime restrictions.

Since regime institutions are the only agencies that have legal rights to do many things in North Korea, it is inevitable that entrepreneurs will bribe regime officials to obtain their licenses, and that officials will run their own private side-businesses to build wealth, causing a breakdown in government authority. The prevalence of corruption corrodes regime control.

Part of the strategy of appeasement practiced by Japan, South Korea, and the U.S. was premised on a belief that once the people of North Korea gained enough personal autonomy and became more aware of the world around them that they would instigate regime change. When the regime feels threatened, however, it becomes more aggressive in enforcing laws and increases public executions, including people in a position of prominence.

The regime has invested a lot of effort into making North Korea the most closed media environment in the world, but compared to two decades ago North Koreans have significantly more access to outside information. This is having a real impact on their views and attitudes.

The regime's information blockade is being broken down by cross-border movement, trade, and new technologies. Marketization is increasing the proliferation of mobile phones, televisions, radios, DVD players, and South Korean dramas and Chinese films to watch on them. It is possible to buy cheap Chinese DVD players for around $20, and DVDs themselves are available for less than a dollar and are commonly shared or even rented. USB drives are also growing in popularity, and are used with computers and the newer DVD players that have a USB input port. This makes it easier to share and watch foreign media without being detected, because USB drives are so easy to conceal.

North Koreans are learning more about the reality of life in the outside world and are discovering the true reasons for their own poverty. Once the truth is known it cannot be unlearned. Exposure to the truth, empowers the North Korean people to think independently from the regime.

A growing segment of the North Korean population engage in market activities representing acts of mass disobedience. They find their interests and needs in opposition to the regime's economic policy, restrictions, and crackdowns. Events such as the 2009 currency revaluation and restrictions on trade directly make people's life more difficult and mean it is increasingly obvious that the country's difficulties are not caused by external hostile forces, but by the regime.

Revolutionary ideology naturally erodes over time, but economic and informational changes have accelerated the growth of cynicism about the regime. Communication of discontent is still risky and limited. The markets have no place in North Korean socialist ideology, and increasing awareness of the outside world contradicts the regime's propaganda. The regime depends on ideology for its legitimacy and are deeply concerned about the role of marketization in breaking the people away from the state both physically and psychologically

As fear becomes a more important factor in maintaining the system, increasing repression only further alienates the public. As the chasm between traditional propaganda and the people's understanding of their reality continues to widen, the regime will be forced to adapt its propaganda to align more with reality and allow a better standard of living in order to maintain long-term power and control, or else see its propaganda become increasingly irrelevant or even counter-productive.

North Koreans who are now in their 20s and early 30s came of age after the collapse of the state-socialist economy an era of marketization and eroding state relevance. Their attitudes, values and even behaviors are significantly different from their parents' and grandparents' generations.

They grew up in an era where people had to fend for themselves. Many of them never relied on the state for work, food, wealth, status, protection, or information. Traditional ideology seems hollow and irrelevant to them, and they are more influenced by foreign media. Many of these young North Koreans show more interest in foreign films, fashions, and music, and feel little attachment to the regime or the leadership; seeing regime officials as takers rather than providers and as the source of problems inside the country. They have less respect for the regime compared to previous generations, and this demographic is going to grow with time. They will be crucial in pushing for change in the future.

Since the famine, North Koreans who were able, fled the country. Over 28,000 North Korean refugees made it all the way to South Korea, with an unknown number still in limbo in China. These refugees play a crucial role as a bridge between the outside world and North Korea:

Many maintain contact with family members still in North Korea, sending information back in and increasing the North Korean people's awareness of the outside world.

Many also send money back to their relatives through brokers. These remittances amount to 10-15 million dollars per year, which is used to buy human security as well as fund smuggling operations and build trade activities, accelerating marketization and creating more space between the people and the regime. Refugees also provide information about the reclusive nation to the outside world.

Since it is illegal to leave the country without state permission, crossing the border is an act of defiance against the repressive government. As more North Koreans become aware of the rising numbers of their fellow countrymen leading better lives in more affluent neighboring countries, this presents a growing challenge to the legitimacy of the North Korean regime.

The regime is rightfully concerned about the effects of the growth of illegal cross-border movement and contact, and has stepped up security and punishments in an attempt to regain control over the border.

Authoritarian regimes often ensure their power by preventing the formation of bonds between the people. To achieve this, they utilize a society-wide system of snitches and informants to keep people's everyday behavior in check, generating a pervading sense of mistrust and fear in the process.

North Koreans are increasingly engaging in shared illegal activities such as illicit business or gathering with small groups of friends to watch foreign films. They are more reliant on each other for goods and information that the regime is either unwilling or unable to provide. Shared participation in illegal activities such as trading banned products or discussion of subversive information leads to mutual dependence, trust building and the normalization of such activities within communities. This in turn encourages further sharing, private political discussion, and the strengthening of bonds between the people. Ultimately this could result in a growing civil space for the people, separate from the regime.

The regime's repressive security apparatus is still too effective to allow any public challenge to the ruling elite. People may be more open with sharing their views, but they are still very cautious, and anything more than very private criticism of the regime within a trusted group of friends or relatives is still too risky.

Social connections may enable people to push back against the regime collectively, on small and localized issues at first. There is evidence that this is already happening.

How We Got to This Point

Understanding the current stand-off with North Korea is challenging. It is important to understand how this untenable situation developed. Korea was absorbed by the Manchu (Qing) dynasty prior to it being colonized by the Japanese in 1910. It is only recently that it has enjoyed self-rule, albeit divided.

According to History of North Korea, 2017, in 1910, Japan annexed and colonized Korea. Koreans remember the Japanese colonial rule as a brutal experience. Resistance groups formed in Korea and China, mostly adopting leftist politics in reaction to the right-wing Japanese administration. Memories of the Japanese Imperial Administration's oppression continue to haunt relations between the people of both Koreas and Japan today. Korea also began to modernize during this period, and the city of Pyongyang became a vibrant center for Christianity and western culture.

Under Japanese rule, Koreans were treated badly. They were enslaved, randomly beaten, killed without consequence and women were forced into sexual slavery and prostitution; some being taken to the Japanese mainland. Japan raped the country of its natural resources. Hostility towards Japan and Japanese from both North and South Koreans remains today.

Following Japan's defeat in 1945 the Soviet Union and United States agreed to split the post-war control of the Korean peninsula between themselves. On August 10, 1945 two young U.S. military officers drew up a line demarcating the U.S. and Soviet occupation zones at the 38th parallel. The divide should have been temporary, but the emergence of the Cold War made this a seminal event. Seeking to ensure the maintenance of their respective influences in Korea, the U.S. and USSR installed leaders sympathetic to their own cause, while mistrust on both sides prevented cooperation on elections that were supposed to choose a leader for the entire peninsula. The United States handed control over the southern half of the peninsula to Syngman Rhee, while the Soviet Union gave Kim Il-Sung power over the north. In 1948, both sides claimed to be the legitimate government and representative of the entire Korean people.

(The Demilitarized Zone, DMZ)

The USSR (Russia and its allied countries) entered the war against Japan only in the final days of the war. They had signed a non-aggression pact with Japan that lasted until the war in Europe was completed. Japan and the

USSR never signed a peace treaty after World War 2, mainly because each country held several islands which were historically territory of the other. In the years after World War 2, a cold war set in between the USSR and the United States. The cold war was fought through proxy wars of conventional military might and ideological influence. Korea found itself a pawn, in a game of chess between these two super-powers.

On August 15, 1948 Syngman Rhee declares the formation of the Republic of Korea in Seoul, claiming jurisdiction over all of Korea. On September 8, 1948 Kim Il-Sung declares the formation of the Democratic People's Republic of Korea in Pyongyang, also claiming jurisdiction over all of Korea.

(North)

In 1950, Kim Il-Sung attempted to unify Korea under his rule through military force, starting the Korean War. By far the most destructive and divisive event in Korean history, the war altered the life of almost every Korean person.

key

Most Americans know very little about the Korean war. The horrors of the war were trivialized in the television show, M.A.S.H. Many North Korean cities, including Pyongyang were reduced to rubble by American bombing. It is estimated that more napalm was used on North Korean cities than in Vietnam. 1,217,000 South Koreans died in this war, with 1 million of those being civilians. 1,004,000 North Koreans were killed, with 600,000 of those being civilians. 600,000 Chinese military members died fighting on the side of North Korea. 36,574 American military troops died fighting for the South and an additional 8000 were never accounted for after the war.

Both sides eventually signed the armistice ending major hostilities in 1953. The DMZ (demilitarized zone) was established at almost the same position as the border before war broke out, separating millions of families caught on opposite sides of the border.

From 1953 to the 1970s North Korea was considered by some outside observers to be a successful state. During this period, many North Koreans were actually better off than their southern brethren.

Part of the initial success of North Korea was due to the unity created by the war and the recovery. The North was also bolstered through investments by its main allies, China and the USSR; both of which share a border with North Korea. The USSR even created a branch extension of its famed Trans-Siberian Railroad which terminates in Pyongyang.

Kim Il-Sung modeled North Korean society along the lines of Juche, North Korea's radically nationalistic ideology promoting Korean autonomy. The state-seized control of all private property and organizations. Officially, everything in the country, from businesses to the clothes on one's back, belongs to the North Korean state. The regime rebuilt Pyongyang as a socialist capital and erected numerous monuments to Kim Il-Sung, part of nationwide efforts to build a cult of personality to secure obedience by the people. The state took control of all media and restricted international travel. Kim Il-Sung also worked constantly to centralize power under the Workers' Party of Korea under his rule, and implemented a perpetual purge to rid the country of potential internal opponents to his rule.

Massive inequalities began to emerge in North Korean society. The regime introduced the songbun system, which is still in place today. Under this system the entire population were sorted into different social classes according to one's perceived loyalty to socialism and the regime. This classification determined the course of people's lives. One's songbun dictates the schools one can attend, the occupations one can be placed in, and even where one can live. At the time, the regime expelled around a quarter of the population of Pyongyang to the outer provinces for being of low songbun.

The regime silenced anyone who opposed the system with extreme prejudice. Free speech became an offense punishable by imprisonment or even death. Worse, when one was arrested, up to three generations of their family would be sent to political prison camps. The regime instructed children to inform on their parents, and neighbors to inform on each other. Under these conditions, the North Korean people became fearful and distrusting of each other.

By the 1970s, the initial gains of postwar reconstruction and modernization had dissipated, and Kim Il-Sung's ideologically driven governance failed to produce prosperity. North Korea was also highly dependent on trade and aid from the Soviet Union and the Eastern bloc, so when the economies of those countries began to decline it greatly affected North Korea's economy. The people's quality of life stagnated in the 1980s and began to decline until the collapse of the USSR in 1991, at which point the North Korean socialist command economy stopped functioning. Poor agricultural policies and environmental mismanagement increased vulnerability to extreme weather conditions and brought increasingly meager crop yields. To make matters worse, the regime had lost allies to fall back on when the economy failed. North Korea's reserves were quickly running out. These were the circumstances the country found itself in when Kim Il-Sung died in 1994.

Kim Jong-Il took power in the post-Cold War era when North Korea was on the brink of disaster. Realizing the need to handle both external and internal threats, Kim Jong-Il instituted a military first policy that prioritized the military and elites over the general population to an even greater extent than before. Many North Koreans blame Kim Jong-Il's leadership for the famine although his policies only exacerbated a crisis that was long in the making.

The economic collapse and subsequent famine in North Korea had its peak in the mid-to-late 1990s. It is estimated that up to one million people died— roughly 5% of the population. Starvation in childhood has stunted the growth of an entire generation of North Koreans. The North Korean government had to lower the minimum required height for soldiers because 145 cm (4 feet 9 inches) was too tall for most 16-17-year old's.

1994 - 198

The official government explanation regarding the cause of the famine was treachery by the United States, Japan, and South Korea. Having no outside news, the

29

population accepted this explanation which increased their hatred of these three countries and shielded the North Korean regime from blame.

The collapse of the command economy led to widespread social changes. The need for food drove the North Korean people away from the regime's control, as when the government stopped providing food, the survivors found other ways to feed themselves. People foraged and sold anything they could to buy food at small, illegal markets that began to spring up, creating a process of bottom-up marketization. Some fled to China, leading to a wave of refugees from North Korea, while information about the outside world slowly began to flow back into the country. Some resorted to prostitution or crime. What was once a highly ordered and controlled society gave way to a disorganized and fluid society, with new independent paths to wealth and power for those who defied the regime and pursued the markets. These social effects would continue even after the worst of the famine had passed.

Always uneasy about the growth of the markets, in late 2009 the regime made their most drastic attempt to restrain the markets to date: a currency reform aimed at wiping out private wealth. The resultant market disruption and rapid inflation reversed the people's hard-won progress, and even regime projects were derailed. North Korean refugees have described this as a watershed moment in their diminishing belief in the regime, with anti-regime sentiment so strong that it even rose to the surface in some communities.

It had been hoped that the regime of Kim Jong Il would either collapse in upon itself or the people would overthrow his regime. The collapse of the Soviet Union brought new hope that people held under repressive governments could and would rise up against their leaders.

In December 2011, Kim Jong-Il died and his son Kim Jong-Un inherited control of the nation. Thought to be just 27 or 28 years old at the time of his succession, Kim Jong-Un was largely unknown to the North Korean people as well as to the outside world. North Koreans that escaped the country in 2011 told us that there had not been a lot of propaganda about Kim Jong-Un during that year. By contrast, Kim Jong-Il was much better known to the North Korean people when he came to power in 1994.

(The Mysterious Leader, Kim Jong Un)

In his first years in power, Kim Jong-Un has implemented a new public relations style that has portrayed him as a modern version of his grandfather, while purging, demoting, and promoting regime officials to secure his power base. The new leadership also moved to crack down on illegal cross-border movement and the inflow of foreign media, increasing repression in the border regions and reducing the number of defectors who managed to make it to South Korea by almost half. Meanwhile, there have been signs of cautious experimentation with economic liberalization to adapt to the reality of the entrenched de facto market economy inside the country.

It is illegal for the North Korean people to leave their country without the regime's permission, and the regime attempts to restrict the people's movement even inside their own country. If you wish to travel to another part of the country, you are supposed to have a specific purpose and obtain permission from your work unit. If you do not live in Pyongyang, the showcase capital where most resources are concentrated, you will likely be denied access. The regime has also forcibly relocated hundreds of thousands of North Koreans to less favorable parts of the country as a form of punishment and political persecution.

It is difficult for anyone living in a free society to understand life in an oppressive society. For North Koreans, it is all they know, and it is difficult for them to understand that life elsewhere is different. Oppression is merely part of daily life. They are used to suffering and sacrifice. They are told that outsiders are evil and will fight fiercely to protect the little they have because it is better than the unknown.

If U.S. news reporters or government officials were to be believed, North Korea is isolated from the rest of the world, and only has diplomatic relations with a handful of pariah states. Most Americans believe this, but it is not true.

North Korea has embassies and diplomatic missions in Africa. Diplomatic offices exist in Algiers, Egypt, Equatorial Guinea, Ethiopia, Ghana, Guinea, Libya, Nigeria, South Africa, Tanzania, and Uganda.

It has embassies and diplomatic missions in the Americas. North Korea has offices in Brazil, Cuba, Mexico, Peru, and Venezuela.

North Korea has diplomatic offices and embassies in Asia. Diplomatic offices exist in China, Vietnam, Nepal, Cambodia, Singapore, Laos, Japan (unofficial), Bangladesh, India, Indonesia, Iran, Kuwait, Malaysia, Mongolia, Pakistan, Syria, Thailand, and Yemen.

It has embassies and diplomatic missions in Europe. It has offices in Austria, Belarus, Bulgaria, Czech Republic, Germany, Italy, Poland, Romania, Russia, Spain, Sweden, Switzerland, and the United Kingdom.

North Korea also has permanent missions with the United Nations in Geneva, Paris, and New York City. Despite a diplomatic presence, this does not necessarily equate with North Korea having good relations with each of these countries.

North Korea is limited in its economic relations with many countries due in part to pressure from the United States to enforce sanctions placed on North Korea by the

United Nations. Should the United States choose to use diplomacy with North Korea, there are many third-party options through which communication can occur.

North Korea continues to have economic and trade ties with China, Russia, Cuba, Venezuela, Vietnam, Laos, Cambodia, Iran, Pakistan, Yemen, and Syria. As China yields to the U.S. demands that it close economic ties with North Korea, Russia has used the opportunity to increase economic ties with North Korea. Fully isolating the country's economy is unlikely, but the North feels the strain.

North Korea blames the United States for its economic and social problems. They are correct to an extent. If the North had the same access to trade and investment as other countries, it would be able to provide a better standard of living for its people. The regime, on the other hand, needs the population to have a perceived enemy in order to unify its people and ensure the preservation of the government.

Having nuclear weapons and threatening to use them is a desperate tactic used to force the United States to consider non-military options in dealing with North Korea, including the lifting of sanctions. The Trump administration is hesitant to reward North Korea's bad behavior. Kim Jong Un has put all his eggs in one basket in the current showdown with the United States. He understands his country cannot survive a U.S. attack but is betting that the U.S. will not be willing to attack if the risk of U.S. civilian casualties is high and thus unacceptable.

China and Russia certainly do not want an increased American presence in Asia. They also do not want to deal with a humanitarian nightmare of millions of refugees flooding over their border regions. Russia and China both understand the dangers of a nuclear North Korea and the tenuous position the United States is currently in. China and Russia pray for a diplomatic solution, although the likelihood of a mutually acceptable agreement between North Korea and the United States is remote. The United States is also aware that the more time that passes, the more technologically advanced North Korea's weapons will become, increasing the urgency of the situation and dangers faced.

It is important to understand the relationships North Korea has with other countries in order to understand how this mysterious hermit state fits into the grander world scheme, the countries it is influenced by, and the countries who are influenced by them.

China

China's primary interest in North Korea is to maintain stability within its sphere of influence. They do not want the daunting burden of a war creating a rush of refugees over its shared border. They do not need economic ties to North Korea but know part of building stability requires an influx of cash into the North. China seems to understand the difficult predicament the United States is in but also wants to lessen rather than increase a U.S. presence in the region. China is dependent on trade with the U.S. and cannot afford to appear unsupportive in other matters.

According to Albert, Eleanor, 2017, *China is North Korea's most important trading partner and main source of food and energy. It has helped sustain Kim Jong-Un's regime, and has historically opposed harsh international sanctions on North Korea in the hope of avoiding regime collapse and a refugee influx across their 870-mile border. Pyongyang's nuclear tests and ongoing missile launches have complicated its relationship with Beijing, which has continued to advocate for the resumption of the Six Party Talks, the multilateral framework aimed at denuclearizing North Korea. A purge of top North Korean officials since its young leader came to power and the assassination of Kim Jong-Nam, Kim Jong-Un's exiled half-brother, in Malaysia also spurred concern from China about the stability and direction of North Korean leadership Alliance Under Stress.*

Kim Jong Nam was the eldest son of Kim Jong Il and was the heir apparent after his father's death. Officially he fell out of favor by embarrassing the regime through his attempt to visit Tokyo Disneyland using a false passport. Kim Jong Nam claimed he actually lost favor by advocating reform in North Korea. In 2017 he was assassinated in Malaysia. It is widely suspected that the exiled Nam was working with the CIA. The chemical weapon attack that killed him was just one of several attempts by North Korean agents to assassinate him.

China's support for North Korea dates back to the Korean War, when its troops flooded the Korean Peninsula to aid its northern ally. Since the war, China has lent political and economic backing to North Korea's leaders: Kim Il-Sung, Kim Jong-Il, and Kim Jong-Un. But strains in the relationship began to surface when Pyongyang tested a nuclear weapon in October 2006 and Beijing supported UN Security Council Resolution 1718, which imposed sanctions on Pyongyang. With this resolution and subsequent ones, Beijing signaled a shift in tone from diplomacy to punishment. After North Korea's most recent nuclear test in September 2017, China called on North Korea to stop taking wrong actions that exacerbate the situation and are not in its own interest. Still, Beijing continues to have significant economic ties with Pyongyang. The two enjoy at best a cold relationship that is likely to worsen.

China is showing signs of frustration with North Korea and while it advocates for diplomacy, it is likely beginning to understand that there is a high probability that war is on the horizon. It has fortified its border and increased military deployments to the border region.

Beijing may be poised to take some limited measures to squeeze Pyongyang economically. China's commerce ministry temporarily suspended coal imports from North Korea in February 2017. State-owned oil giant, China National Petroleum Corporation, suspended fuel sales to North Korea in June 2017, citing concerns that North Korea would fail to pay the company. As of September 2017, media reports cited efforts by Chinese banks, including China Construction Bank, Bank of China, and the Agricultural Bank of China, to restrict the financial activities of North Korean individuals and businesses. The measures include closing some accounts, freezing others, and banning the opening of new ones. Some regional experts say such actions may suggest that the Chinese regime is losing patience with Pyongyang, while others say that these shifts by Beijing are merely tactical.

China provides North Korea with most of its food and energy supplies and accounts for more than 90 percent of North Korea's total trade volume.

In September 2015, the two countries opened a bulk cargo and container shipping route to boost North Korea's export of coal to China and China established a high-speed rail route between the Chinese border city of Dandong and Shenyang, the provincial capital of China's northeastern Liaoning province. In October 2015, the Guomenwan border trade zone opened in Dandong with the intention of boosting bilateral economic linkages, much like the Rason economic zone and the Sinujiu special administrative zone established in North Korea in the early 1990s and 2002, respectively. Dandong is a critical hub for trade, investment, and tourism for the *two neighbors. A new $350 million bridge over the Yalu River to connect the two cities, intended to open in 2014, remains incomplete across the North Korean border, a symbol of cooling relations between Beijing and Pyongyang. Still, North Korea's dependence on China continues to grow. Moreover, established informal trade along the China-North Korea border in items such as fuel, seafood, silkworms, and cell phones signals that despite stricter sanctions, smugglers are likely to continue to operate.*

Beijing also provides aid directly to Pyongyang, primarily in food and energy assistance. China, Japan, South Korea, and the United States have provided more than 75 percent of food aid to North Korea since 1995, but donations from all countries except for China have shrunk significantly since the collapse of the Six Party Talks in 2009. North Korea, whose famine in the 1990s killed an untallied amount of people, has repeatedly faced extensive droughts and severe flooding, which seriously damage harvests, threatening the country's food supply. UN agencies estimate that up to 70 percent of the population, or eighteen million people, are undernourished and food insecure. There is also concern about the distribution of aid in North Korea, particularly since China has no system to monitor shipments.

China regards stability on the Korean peninsula as its primary interest. Its support for North Korea ensures a buffer between China and the democratic South, which is home to around twenty-nine thousand U.S. troops and marines. While the Chinese certainly would prefer that North Korea not have nuclear weapons, their greatest fear is regime collapse.

Beijing has consistently urged world powers not to push Pyongyang too hard, for fear of precipitating the leadership's collapse and triggering dangerous military action. "Once a war really happens, the result will be nothing but multiple loss. No one can become a winner," said Chinese Foreign Minister Wang Yi in April 2017, urging the United States and North Korea to show restraint.

Americans are very distractible with multiple-media choices, social media, video games, and the majority of the American population is woefully unaware of either events occurring in the world, or the true dangers those events may bring. Because the American mainland has only been minimally impacted by war, there is a false sense of security that the military will be able prevent all future attacks as well. North Korea has threatened the U.S. in the past, but truly posed little risk to any country outside of its immediate proximity. Unaware of the full extent of the North Korean threat, Americans tend to wonder why the U.S. military has not simply attacked and wiped out the threat posed by the hermit nation. The military knows that the U.S. will win any war but the cost of war in terms of property, lives, and the future of strategic alliances will be enormous. The United States knows there will be no way to ensure that there will not be casualties within the American civilian population. North Korea and every country within close proximity have experienced war on their home territories and desperately want diplomacy to work. China, which is experiencing economic and political prominence

40

is especially invested in preventing a war that will impact the positive changes occurring there.

The specter of hundreds of thousands of North Korean refugees flooding into China is also a worry for Beijing. "Instability generated on the peninsula could cascade into China, making China's challenge of providing for its own people that much more difficult," says Mike Mullen, former chairman of the U.S. Joint Chiefs of Staff. The refugee issue is already a problem for China: Beijing's promise to repatriate North Koreans escaping across the border has consistently triggered condemnation from human rights groups. Beijing began constructing a barbed-wire fence more than a decade ago to prevent migrants from crossing, but the International Rescue Committee estimates thirty to sixty thousand North Korean refugees live in China, though some nongovernmental organizations believe the total to be more than two hundred thousand. The majority of refugees first make their way to China before moving to other parts of Asia, including South Korea. However, tightened border controls under Kim Jong-Un have decreased the outflow of refugees.

Though Beijing favors a stable relationship with Pyongyang, it has also bolstered its ties with Seoul. China's Xi Jinping has met with South Korean President Moon Jae-in and his predecessor Park Geun-hye on several occasions, while he has yet to visit or receive the North's Kim. China was South Korea's top trading partner in 2016 and the destination for a quarter of the South's exports. Meanwhile, South Korea ranked fourth among

China's trade partners. Recently China has taken retaliatory measures against South Korean businesses to oppose the deployment of the U.S. missile defense system in South Korea's eastern province of North Gyeongsang.

Experts say China has also been ambivalent on the question of its commitment to defend North Korea in case of military conflict. The 1961 Sino-North Korean Treaty of Friendship, Cooperation, and Mutual Assistance, up for renewal in 2021, says China is obliged to intervene against unprovoked aggression. But Bonnie Glaser of the Center for Strategic and International Studies says the Chinese government has tried to persuade North Korean leaders to revoke the clause that would force Beijing to come to Pyongyang's defense. The Brookings Institution's Jeffrey Bader describes the alliance between Beijing and Pyongyang as "a thing of the past," saying that "the two enjoy at best a cold relationship that is likely to worsen." Beijing has also intimated that if Pyongyang initiates conflict, it would not abide by its treaty obligation.

China's added a qualification to its commitment to protect North Korea after Pyongyang's most recent provocations. If North Korea attacks first, China will not intervene. This qualification is significant to the U.S. because it does not want to be in a position of direct military conflict with China. Without China's support, the North would have quickly lost the Korean War. China lost 600,000 soldiers fighting in support of the North. This number of casualties is almost 20 times the number of Americans who died supporting the South.

If the United States attacks North Korea first, China states it will honor its agreement to protect the North. The U.S. does not want China involved in any Korean conflict for military, economic, and political reasons. China's statement is likely playing a large role in holding both sides in the current stalemate.

Despite the stalemate, the U.S. still must project a confident military stance in the region in order to reassure its allies that they will be protected. It must wait for North Korea's provocations to escalate or North Korea to back down. Neither situation is likely to occur. This increases the likelihood that the U.S. could stage a false flag event to start the war or worst-case scenario, a third party such as Russia or a terrorist organization could attack the U.S. or allied assets which will be blamed on North Korea and provoke a horrific war.

The United States has pushed North Korea to irreversibly give up its nuclear weapons program in return for aid, diplomatic benefits, and normalization of relations. But experts say Washington and Beijing, while sharing the goal of denuclearizing North Korea, have different views on how to reach it. The United States values using pressure to force North Korea to negotiate on its nuclear weapons program, while China advocates for the resumption of multilateral talks and what it called a "freeze for freeze," a freeze in military exercises by the United States and its allies for a freeze in North Korea's nuclear and missile testing. Ultimately, for Beijing; stability on the Korean Peninsula has always been prioritized over denuclearization.

Washington has also tried to pressure Beijing to lean more heavily on Pyongyang. U.S. presidential executive orders and congressional moves impose sanctions on countries, firms, or individuals contributing to North Korea's ability to finance nuclear and missile development; some measures targeted North Korean funds in Chinese banks, while others focus on its mineral and metal export industries, which make up an important part of trade with China. Washington deployed a missile defense system known as the Terminal High Altitude Area Defense, or THAAD, in 2017 to boost regional security, though Beijing strongly condemns the move and sees it as a threat to Chinese national security.

China's economic progress is due to free trade with the United States and the domestic security of China is dependent on this relationship continuing. China is not reliant on trade with North Korea but engaging with the North helps prevent a humanitarian crisis that would impact the border shared by both countries. If push came to shove, China would protect its internal and economic security and side with the United States but will likely seek other U.S. concessions in the region

The administration of President Donald J. Trump has shaken up U.S. policy toward North Korea. Officials have stated that "all options are on the table," alluding to the possibility of preemptive military strikes to thwart Pyongyang's nuclear tests and development. Trump has also warned that Washington will be prepared to take unilateral action against Pyongyang if Beijing remains unwilling to exert more pressure on its neighbor. "If China is not going to solve North Korea, we will," Trump said in an April 2017 interview with the Financial Times. Going even further, Trump told the UN General Assembly in September 2017 that the United States would "have no choice but to totally destroy North Korea," if it was forced to defend itself or its allies. The U.S. military has stepped up joint exercises with Japan and South Korea and has periodically dispatched U.S. carrier strike groups near North Korea as a show of force.

The world has grown used to hearing threatening rhetoric from North Korea. The North has used this as a strategy to get rewards for calming the rhetoric. The cycle is endless, threats by the North have previously been met with increased aid from Japan, South Korea, and the U.S. President Trump is taking a different strategy with the hope of getting a different result.

Still, the United States appears more interested in leveraging China's economic influence over North Korea. The U.S. Treasury has imposed some secondary sanctions on both Chinese and Russian entities. Some analysts worry that such economic pressures and further alienation of Pyongyang could embolden the Kim regime to resort to rash military action. Others question the effectiveness of sanctions in getting China to bring North Korea to the negotiating table. North Korea has vowed that the country's nuclear weapons program will never be up for negotiation.

The situation is very complex and there is no assurance that any one path will be successful. A multi-pronged approach is currently occurring which includes economic, diplomatic, political and military options.

The North Korean leadership has convinced itself (if not others) that its existence as an autonomous state derives directly from its possession of nuclear weapons. Though China may be unhappy about North Korea's nuclear brinkmanship, analysts say it will avoid moves that could cause a sudden regime collapse.

Even as China signals that it will toughen its stance toward North Korea, though stopping short of challenging its survivability, there is mounting skepticism that China alone can resolve the North Korea problem. Chinese officials have emphasized that they do not hold the key to the issue. Some analysts say that China's tightening of economic ties is unlikely to deter Kim's nuclear ambitions, while others say the North Korean leader no longer cares what China thinks of its actions.

North Korea's nuclear program is becoming increasingly problematic for China's desire to maintain regional stability.

Russia

The Kim dynasty in North Korea was created by the USSR (Russia and its satellite countries). While never fully absorbed into the Soviet Union, the government was designed, and continues to follow Stalinist doctrine. Korea was not meant to remain bifurcated but remains so today due to the division created by the cold war. Russia shares a small border with North Korea. Despite Russia no longer being communist, it retains strong ties to North Korea and helps keep the Kim regime in power.

The Soviets have long denied their material support of North Korea during the Korean War, but it is known that they provided medical supplies, aircraft and pilots to the North. Soviet pilots participating in the campaign were forbidden to speak any language other than basic Korean over their radios but often resorted to Russian when stressed or swearing. Since officially the USSR was not identified as a belligerent, it is unknown how many Russians may have died in the war.

> According to Rinna, Anthony, 2017, *Despite the North Korean state ideology of juche ("self-reliance"), the DPRK has long depended on either China or Russia as its most important international partner. In light of China's recent curtailment of its support for North Korea, coinciding with an uptick in North Korea-Russia relations, a common supposition is that Russia is once again taking pride of place in North Korea's international collaborators. There is little doubt that Russia is making sincere attempts at building a partnership with North Korea. North Korea and Russia declared 2015 to be a "Year of Friendship" between the two countries. The two*

countries have also signed various agreements, such as a treaty that will make it easier for Russia to return North Korean defectors to the DPRK.

When the Russians annexed Crimea, Western countries imposed major sanctions on trade with Russia. Rather than yield to western demands, Vladimir Putin turned to Asia to develop enhanced trade partnerships. While Europe would pay a premium price for the same products, the sanctions made them inconsistent partners. China welcomed the additional trade with Russia across its vast shared border but purchased Russian products at a greatly reduced price as compared to what Europeans would pay. As China yields to pressure from the United States and others to isolate North Korea through sanctions, Russia is eyeing the trade vacancy created as an opportunity to increase trade with North Korea, selling goods at a premium price. Russia already has a transportation system (a spur of the famed Trans-Siberian Railroad) which extends to Pyongyang.

The idea that Russia is once again superseding China as North Korea's major international patron bodes well when viewed through the prism of North Korea's Cold War-era tactics of playing China and the USSR off of each other. Likewise, increased Russian support for North Korea coincides with the paradigm that Russia would back countries that are opposed to US power for the sake of diminished American clout in foreign affairs. Nevertheless, the realities of new developments in North Korea-Russia relations contrast with the Cold War era, when Russia (then, the Soviet Union) had no diplomatic ties with South Korea.

The current nature of DPRK-Russia ties is not based on ideology as in the past. Russia often touts the creation of a "multi-polar world", and many official statements on Russia's relations with China allude to this as being an important part of Sino-Russian relations. Yet Russia's main purpose in its ties with the DPRK are driven more by a Russian desire to develop and securitize its Far Eastern regions. Russia, in particular, values its geographic access to North Korea as a way to reach broader global markets through the Greater Tumen Initiative, and utilizes its cordial relations with Pyongyang to strive for a non-military solution to the North Korean nuclear standoff.

Unlike in the past, Russia now has diplomatic relations with the South. South Korea has greater economic resources than the North and Russia would like to build a lasting trade relationship with the South. In order to protect this relationship, any assistance given to the North will probably be done quietly. The secret nature of their trade and other involvements in the North makes assessing the strengths and weaknesses of the North more difficult since the United States and others cannot know for certain whether North Korean sanctions are working.

One of the current pressing issues that reveals the complexity of Russia's policy toward North Korea is the deployment of the US military's Terminal High Altitude Area Defense (THAAD) to South Korea. Russia has vowed to coordinate a response to THAAD with China, yet Russia has taken a divergent approach from China in dealing with the missile defense system as far as policy toward the Korean Peninsula is concerned. Specifically, Russia has been cautious about jeopardizing its relationship with South Korea, a sworn foe of the DPRK and staunch ally of the United States.

As counter-intuitive as it seems, rather than bolstering DPRK-Russia ties based on a common cause, THAAD reveals the limits of North Korean-Russian cooperation. Russian diplomats and lawmakers have been vocal about their opposition to THAAD and its potential consequences for Northeast Asian security. The Russian foreign ministry has declared that THAAD will complicate the resolution of the ongoing Korean security crisis, while Konstantin Kosachev of Russia's Federation Council asserts that THAAD will provide North Korea with an incentive to continue its nuclear program. Such statements from Moscow indicate serious Russian apprehension about a nuclear-armed North Korea.

The collapse of the USSR came as a surprise to much of the world. The speed of the breakup was even more shocking. While people in the west exhaled, feeling that the world was now safer, this period was actually much more dangerous. Nuclear weapons and nuclear scientists were scattered through the defunct USSR, not simply Russia proper. The weapons needed to be relocated to Russia proper or pose a threat to Russia by those angry at the prior Soviet occupation. Weapons also posed a threat to the world as the cash strapped former soviet countries in which they were located could sell them or the technology to build them to outside countries. Scientists with the knowledge to create these weapons could also relocate to countries offering the best compensation and standard of living. It is quite possible that the technology North Korea now possesses originated from sources linked to the breakup of the USSR.

> *Although North Korea and Russia have expressed a desire for closer military engagement, nothing substantial has yet come to fruition, particularly nothing that could be seen as opposing South Korea. Rather than opposing South Korea, Russia's general response to THAAD has been to focus more directly on its implications for Russia's ties with the United States. Viktor Ozerov, chairman of the Federation Council's defense committee has asserted that THAAD's installation in Korea may be sufficient grounds for Russia to withdraw from the New Strategic Arms Reduction Treaty (New START). Ozerov indicated that the Russian General Staff was conducting an analysis of the feasibility of this course of action.*

While the deployment of THAAD in South Korea may not be related to US-Russia relations it does allow the

US the potential of being able to shoot down Russian missiles during the early launch stages, theoretically giving the US an advantage in the event of all out nuclear war. In reality, the system is unproven, and would likely only be effective in a limited missile exchange. The theory of Mutually Assured Destruction (MAD) states that in the event of a nuclear confrontation between the US and Russia, each country would attack with its full capacity and neither would survive. While THAAD may prove to be an effective defense against a small-scale attack, if Russia were to launch all missiles against the U.S. the THAAD system would have negligible impact.

Russia's ability or unwillingness to pressure South Korea regarding THAAD is also compounded by a strong Russian desire to increase commercial ties with South Korea. Immediately at the end of the Cold War, the USSR for all intents and purposes turned its back on North Korea, seeing continued partnership with the Communist state as being of little benefit for a Soviet rump state; the Russian Federation, seeking to rebuild itself. Russia promptly established diplomatic relations with South Korea. After a somewhat clumsy start to Russia's relations with both Koreas, Russia has since pursued a policy of balancing its interests with both countries on the Korean Peninsula.

Russia's main interests in engaging North Korea are economic, border security and limiting American influence in the region. The countries no longer forge a relationship based upon share ideology.

Russian military expert Alexei Leonkov warns that Russia may limit its economic cooperation with South

Korea in response to THAAD. Such a course of action, however, does not coincide with recent developments in Russia's ties with South Korea, which have generally been quite positive. In the autumn of 2016, during a plenary session of the Eastern Economic Forum, South Korea's then-president Park Geun-hye announced that Russia and South Korea were considering implementing a free trade agreement between the Republic of Korea and the Eurasian Economic Union. From the Russian end, the Russian ambassador to South Korea, Alexei Timonin, praised South Korea as an important partner for Russia, and expressed hopes that the two sides could continue their partnership despite disagreements over THAAD.

Russia, therefore, values North Korea as a partner, but must approach the DPRK with a degree of caution. As the standoff over THAAD worsens, several factors, including developments in South Korea's domestic politics, will affect the future

course of North Korea-Russia relations. Nevertheless, Russia's ties to South Korea will continue to be one of the biggest factors in determining the course and nature of DPRK-Russia relations. As much as Russia values its partnership with North Korea, it takes care not to neglect its relations with the Republic of Korea. Thus, in order for Russia to realize its broader goals in Northeast Asia, Russia must continue to deal with two different political entities on the Korean Peninsula, a less-than-ideal situation for Russia.

If the US were to fully engage in a war in North Korea, the US would be limited in its ability to influence conflicts elsewhere in the world. Russia would likely become emboldened to exude its influence in other regions. Russia is being pressured by ill-conceived UN sanctions and it is possible, however unlikely, that Russia could fake a North Korean attack, thus prompting an all-out conflict, in order to tie up US resources in one region of the world thus allowing Russia free reign over other regions.

really?

Preserving the rule of a dictatorship requires a common enemy for the population to focus on. North Korea was born a Stalinist state, during the cold war. Anti-American sentiments were a common thread within the Soviet Union and those countries which aligned themselves through ideology.

North Koreans are told Americans are evil from a very young age. They are told America started the Korean war, although the North attacked the South. Kim Jong Sung is depicted as the warrior savior of the North from the Japanese, although he spent most of the war, safely protected in a village in the Soviet Union.

According to History of North Korea, 2017, *some historians claim that the U.S. military dropped more napalm on urban centers in Korea than Vietnam. The bombing campaigns reduced Pyongyang to rubble, and North Korea's population was reduced by 10%.*

Until recently, America looked at North Korea as little more than an irritation. It had neither the financial nor military ability to pose a serious threat. The situation became worse for North Korea when the USSR collapsed and was no longer able to provide gratuitous financial support to the hermit nation. Although hidden from Russian view, the collapse of the USSR is often depicted with intense contempt within North Korea.

North Korea knew it could no longer rely on either military or financial support from Russia. As the population suffered through famine and isolation, the rhetoric against the US increased. The regime was at risk both due to internal struggles of the people and the inevitability that news of the far more powerful USSR had collapsed would further empower those inside North Korea who aspired to change. The importance of the US being seen as a villain increased, as did the need to make public examples of those in North Korea who threatened the stability of the regime by advocating change.

According to North Korea News, 2014, North Korea is one of the most anti-American countries on Earth. If you open a North Korean newspaper you will not struggle to find references to U.S. imperialism, the U.S. "occupation" of "South" Korea and, of course, U.S. militarism. Added to that, everything from North Korean reference texts and encyclopedias, to posters and parades are full of negative references to the American army and its "evil" government. You would struggle to find any country outside certain parts of the Middle East that expends quite so much energy and ink on anti-American crowd-baiting.

Many self-critical Americans, as well as those who do not like the United States, are quick to blame America itself for creating the people who hate it. An endless list of grievances can be drawn up for the crimes (real and alleged) that the United States has to answer for. But crimes themselves do not fully explain why people hate America, and for that matter why the North Korean government is so very determined to make its people hate America.

People hate America and governments mobilize their people under the anti-American banner for many reasons, but in North Korea the reasons are political.

During the Korean War, the United States dropped countless bombs on North Korea. The Korean War was also one of the first times the United States used napalm against one of its enemies (Japan seems to have the dubious "honor" of being the first during the Second World War). Napalm is a very effective way to immobilize your enemy in a very painful and nasty manner, burning them alive, and it is indiscriminate, i.e. when used near civilians expect massive collateral damage.

Under any circumstance, the use of napalm is horrific. In Vietnam it was predominantly used to clear forests and on known military targets. In Korea, it was often used in urban areas where civilian casualties were likely to occur. Asking older Koreans to forget about this atrocity would be like expecting Americans to forget about Pearl Harbor or the 911 attacks. While the younger generation may be more forgiving, there is genuine hatred of America amongst the older North Koreans which the North Korean regime was able to capitalize on through propaganda. The younger generation, however, have had greater exposure to the outside world and show more openness to things outside of North Korea. While a full-on conflict with the United States would devastate the North, a limited conflict would allow the North Korean regime to regain control of is younger generation.

It should be remembered that the North Korean state was very much the aggressor in the Korean conflict; the North Korean People's Army (KPA) invaded South Korea on June 25, 1950. It was only thanks to the swift intervention of the UN forces, led by the United States, that South Korea survived. But we should also not forget that UN forces under U.S. direction chose to invade the North after they had been successfully repelled the KPA from South Korean territory. This invasion, followed by years of attrition warfare and regular U.S. bombing raids on the North meant that many in the North, as well as China (a key participant in the war), associated the United States with death and brutality. In all, well over a million North Korean civilians (in a population of around 10 million) are believed to have died in the Korean War.

The original Korean mission was to liberate South Korea from the North. The continued attack on the North after the liberation of the South could be seen by some as action beyond the scope of the mandate. A contemporary example of moving beyond the mandate occurred during Operation Desert Storm. The mandate was to liberate Kuwait, but the U.S. attempted to move beyond that mandate and conquered the southern half of Iraq before yielding to global pressure. After the carnage committed by the U.S. on retreating Iraqi troops on the "highway of hell", international pressure bore down on the United States to operate under the rules of the mandate and leave Iraq.

From all of this it is easy to conclude that North Koreans hate America because America violated the rules of war, and that North Korean government propaganda represents the popular will of the North Korean people. The argument goes that Presidents Truman and Eisenhower, by authorizing massive bombing raids that killed thousands of civilians gave the Korean people, both North Koreans and South Koreans who think critically about the U.S. role in their own society and the Korean War, a reason to hate them, the U.S. government in general, and perhaps even the American people. Such conclusions, though, are hopelessly simplistic and do not help us understand the real roots of the North Korean government's "hatred" of America, or rather, their burning desire to ensure that their people do.

Vietnam is the perfect counterpoint to North Korea: The Vietnamese people are not united in their hatred of all things American, the Vietnamese government does not mobilize their people for annual "Days of Struggle against U.S. Imperialism" on the anniversary of the start of the Vietnam War (as the North Korean government does on June 25). Nor does Hanoi play host to regular parades in which posters depicting U.S. soldiers being bayoneted are held aloft by the citizens of that great metropolis. The Vietnamese government is so keen to forgive, while the North Koreans are all too eager not to.

The Vietnam War was actually very similar to the Korean War; ironically, the major difference was that it was provoked, by the United States. The Vietnam War began with the Gulf of Tonkin incident of 1965, in which North Vietnamese ships were alleged to have attacked the USS Maddox in international waters (an act of war). In fact, no such incident ever took place, but the people up top were not very interested in the reality on the ground; what they were really interested in was finding a means by which to make sure that communism did not spread from North Vietnam throughout Southeast Asia.

It is also worth noting that the Vietnam War went on for more than 10 years, whereas the Korean War was over in little over three. The Vietnam War also ended more recently in the mid-1970s, while the Korean War was over by 1953, more than six decades ago. The Vietnamese government is keen to forgive, while the North Koreans are not.

Vietnamese see U.S. economic power as a means by which to become rich themselves and U.S. military power as a means of warding off the ever-present threat of China. North Koreans continue to be subjected to regular harangues about the evils of American imperialism but their former communist brothers-in-arms in Vietnam are in the firm embrace of an alliance with the United States.

The U.S. military presence in South Korea may make some North Korean policymakers nervous, but that is not the principal reason for anti-American hysteria. The real reason is that the North Korean government needs its people to see it as a protector against the United States and their "flunkies" in "South" Korea. This external threat is one of the main ways in which the North Korean government seeks to justify its existence to its people. South Korea is, in North Korean propaganda, a place contaminated by American cultural influence, a place yearning to be free of American military occupation, while the North is a pure Korean bastion free of American culture.

Japan

North Korea's closest (geographically) neighbor, apart from those with which it shares a border, is Japan. The closest point between the two countries is 31 miles. The proximity is exasperated by North Korea's territorial water claims differing from those established by the international community. At different points in time, North Korea has tried to claim 50-200 miles of territorial waters. These claims were rebuffed by the international community who state the norm as 3 miles. By special agreement, it has been accepted that North Korean waters extend for 12 nautical miles.

Japan is also Americanized. After the post-World War 2 occupation, the Japanese came to embrace American culture from baseball to bourbon; skyscrapers to fast food; jeans to pop music. Given its proximity to North Korea, Due to its proximity, Japan has more power than the U.S. to influence North Korean culture which makes it a threat to the hermit nation.

Japan was demilitarized after World War 2 and became dependent upon protection through numerous American military bases. After 72 years, Japan has taken a renewed interest in taking care of its own military needs. The U.S. sees Japan as a loyal ally and no longer a threat. The burden on America to continue to protect Japan is expensive and cannot go on forever. North Korea's greatest fear is a militarized Japan. The North's actions, however, have sharply edged Japan in that direction.

According to Blomquist & Wertz, 2017, *Japan and Korea share a history of exchange and conflict dating back nearly two millennia, and Japan's 1910-*

1945 period of colonial rule in Korea continues to cast a long shadow over its relationships on both halves of the Peninsula. Since the end of World War II and the division of Korea, relations between Japan and North Korea have been mostly defined by tension and distrust, punctuated by occasional periods of tentative engagement. The ethnic Korean community in Japan has played an important role in this relationship, with the pro-North Korean organization, Chongryon, acting as an unofficial North Korean embassy in Japan.

North Korean agents abducted Japanese citizens from Japan. Japan recognized 17 abductees while North Korea eventually admitted to 13. There may have been hundreds of victims though. Non-Japanese citizens, including 9 Europeans have also been abducted by North Korea.

Most of the abducted were young and were taken to teach Japanese language and culture at North Korean spy schools. Older victims were usually killed immediately so that North Korean agents could assume their identities. Others may have been kidnapped for witnessing activities of North Korean agents in Japan. American's, Dutch, Lebanese, Yugoslavians, French, South Koreans, Italians, Jordanians, Malaysians, and Singaporeans have also been abducted for similar purposes.

Japan's current priorities regarding North Korea center around the issue of North Korea's past abductions of Japanese citizens, and concerns over North Korea's nuclear and missile programs. North Korea, which frequently issues strong criticisms of Japanese policies, has prioritized in various rounds of dialogue with Tokyo the normalization of relations between the two countries and receiving financial compensation for perceived historical injustices.

After the Russo-Japanese War in 1905, Japan assumed de facto control over Korea, formally annexing the Peninsula in 1910. As part of an effort to build an economically self-sufficient empire, Japan invested into Korea's industrialization, establishing most of the heavy industry in the northern half of the Peninsula. Korea supplied Japan with industrial equipment such as steel, tools, machines, and chemicals, as well as foodstuffs. However, the benefits of this increasing economic productivity did not reach the majority of the Korean population.

Japan implemented harsh and restrictive policies towards the Korean people throughout the colonial period, with policies of forcible assimilation hitting a peak as Japan expanded its empire during the 1930s and 40s. As Japan waged war throughout Asia and the Pacific, its government and military began to recruit Koreans (often coercively) to work at jobs left behind by Japanese conscripts, as well as Korean women to serve soldiers at military installations across its empire. Tokyo also sought to forcibly assimilate Koreans into Japanese culture by assigning Koreans Japanese names, promoting the exclusive use of the Japanese language, and banning the teaching of Korea's language and history.

The circumstances surrounding Japanese colonial rule prompted various forms of Korean resistance, including a major series of protests for independence that began on March 1, 1919. Left-wing resistance groups formed during the 1930s among the ethnic Korean communities in Manchuria. One of these guerilla groups was led by Kim Il-Sung, who was forced into exile in the Soviet Union in 1941 after a series of Japanese counterinsurgency campaigns.

The left-wing resistance movement made acceptance of the USSR influenced Stalinist government imposed on North Koreans seem like a logical progression in claiming independence from Japanese rule. Although the implication of communist rule may not have been fully understood, the movement was powerful enough to rid the North of Imperial Japanese occupation, and that was good enough for the masses.

Immediately after Japan's defeat in World War II, the United States and the Soviet Union divided the Korean Peninsula at the 38th parallel, leading three years later to the establishment of the Democratic People's Republic of Korea (DPRK) led by Kim Il- Sung in the north and the Republic of Korea (ROK) led by Syngman Rhee in the south. War between the two Koreas broke out on June 25, 1950, as the North Korean People's Army invaded the South. The U.S., which led the Allied occupation of Japan from 1945 to 1952, used Japan as a major logistical base for its intervention in the Korean War; a contingent of Japanese sailors also conducted minesweeping operations in the waters around the North Korean coast.

At the end of World War II, over two million Koreans were living in Japan. The majority returned to South Korea after the war; however, 600,000 Koreans remained in Japan. These "Zainichi Koreans" often experienced systematic discrimination in Japan, losing their Japanese nationality and facing barriers to formal employment. Those who identified as North Korean or sympathized with the DPRK established Chongryon, the General Association of Korean Residents in Japan, with the assistance of North Korea in 1955. Chongryon, also known as Chosen Soren in Japanese, has functioned as a network and advocacy organization for pro-DPRK Koreans in Japan, and has served as a portal for trade with North Korea; it has also acted as an unofficial North Korean Embassy in Tokyo.

Between 1959 and 1984, the Chongryon facilitated the "repatriation" of more than 93,000 Korean residents in Japan to North Korea. (Most of these migrants were originally from the southern half of the Peninsula.) Once in North Korea, the "returnees" frequently faced economic hardship, suspicion from security agencies, and limited ability to communicate with relatives back in Japan. Several thousand migrants were Japanese citizens. These included the Japanese spouses of ethnic Koreans, the children of ethnically-mixed unions, and ethnic Koreans who had gone through the lengthy process of obtaining citizenship. Migration slowed as economic conditions worsened in North Korea, and as news about realities on the ground there filtered back to the Korean community in Japan.

Chongryon established a significant presence in Japan by creating an ethnic Korean enclave in Japanese society. The organization established and operated its own businesses, banks, schools,

66

hospitals, and newspaper. Prior to restrictions being imposed in the 2000s, Chongryon operated commercial vessels transporting goods between Japan and North Korea with few restrictions or inspections, while also remitting earnings from Koreans in Japan to their families in North Korea. From 1992 until the imposition of sanctions in 2006, a large ferry and cargo ship, the Mangyongbong-92, sailed regularly between the Japanese city of Niigata and Wonsan, a city on North Korea's eastern coast. Chongryon also established a network of pachinko parlors in Japan, which allegedly served as a front for gambling and illicit activities.

Credit unions associated with Chrongryon, known as chogins, reportedly played a major role in raising and sending money to North Korea, making false loans or engaging in other fraudulent practices in order to illegally remit funds. In the late 1990s, several of the loosely-regulated chogins went into bankruptcy, leading to their consolidation and a multi-billion-dollar bailout of their depositors by the Japanese government. Japanese authorities subsequently cracked down on these financial institutions, putting their activities under greater scrutiny and arresting former executives for embezzlement.

During the Cold War era, the intense competition between the two Koreas for domestic and international legitimacy shaped Japan's relations with the Peninsula. Although Japan developed informal diplomatic and trade links with North Korea through organizations including the Chongryon and

67

the Japan Socialist Party, it established diplomatic relations only with the South. Tokyo's 1965 agreement on normalization of relations with Seoul provided an $800 million aid package and acknowledgement of the ROK as "the only lawful government in Korea." However, as the South Korean government adopted a policy of Nordpolitick in the late 1980s, seeking to improve relations with communist countries including North Korea, an opportunity opened for Japan to discuss establishing formal ties with the DPRK.

In 1990, a top Liberal Democratic Party official, Shin Kanemaru, traveled to Pyongyang to begin discussions on normalization of relations. Although the government of Japan retracted Kanemaru's initial offer to provide compensation for the division of Korea, this outreach continued through eight rounds of subsequent Foreign Ministry talks. By 1992, however, this process stalled due to the mounting North Korean nuclear crisis as well as the DPRK's unwillingness to address the abductions of Japanese citizens by North Korean agents.

Tokyo's relations with Pyongyang improved somewhat after the U.S. and DPRK signed the Agreed Framework on North Korea's nuclear program in 1994: Japan agreed to help finance the Korean Peninsula Energy Development Organization (KEDO) project resulting from the agreement, and also donated over 500,000 tons of food to the DPRK for famine relief in 1995-96. Several Japanese women who had moved to North Korea with their spouses as part of the Chongryon "repatriation" were also allowed by Pyongyang to return to Japan to visit their families during this period. However, after North Korea's launch of a two-stage Taepodong-1 missile in August 1998, which overflew Japanese territory without prior warning, Japan issued sanctions on North Korea and temporarily froze its funding to KEDO.

Dialogue resumed in 2000, as Japan resumed food aid to North Korea and Pyongyang engaged in negotiations with Washington over its missile program. Over three rounds of talks, Japan intimated that it would be willing to offer the DPRK an economic assistance package, similar to that offered to the ROK in 1965, in lieu of reparations and upon normalization of relations. (The package would reportedly have been between $5 and $10 billion). However, disagreement over whether to refer to the funds as an 'economic assistance package' (Japan) or 'reparations/compensation' (North Korea), as well as continuing disputes over the abduction, nuclear, and missile issues, led to an impasse in negotiations.

Following a two-year hiatus in official talks, Prime Minister Junichiro Koizumi met Kim Jong-Il in Pyongyang in September 2002 in the first meeting of the two countries' heads of state. These talks produced the "Japan-DPRK Pyongyang Declaration," under which North Korea agreed to extend the missile test moratorium that began in 1999, fulfill its commitments regarding its nuclear program, and continue to pursue bilateral negotiations toward normalization. In return,

Koizumi apologized for the Japanese occupation of Korea and reiterated Japan's commitment to provide the North with economic assistance upon the normalization of relations. During this summit, in a radical shift from the North's previous stance, Kim Jong-Il also acknowledged and apologized for the past abductions of Japanese citizens by North Korean agents.

During the 1970s and 1980s, North Korea performed covert operations to kidnap Japanese citizens, conducting these operations for a variety of reasons. Until 2002, however, North Korea adamantly denied any involvement when confronted by Japan about the issue. Japan has officially identified cases of abductions of its citizens by North Korean agents. While Japanese organizations involved with the issue have estimated that the total number is closer to 100, the precise figure is unknown.

In his statement at the 2002 summit with Prime Minister Koizumi, Kim Jong-Il reportedly said that the issue "is regretful and I want to frankly apologize," and that those responsible for the kidnappings would be "sternly punished." North Korea eventually admitted to the abduction of 13 victims, claiming that five were alive and eight had died from various natural causes or accidents. However, some of the reported deaths appeared to take place under suspicious circumstances, and could not be confirmed. In addition, North Korea denied knowledge of any other abductees.

Kim Jong-Il's acknowledgement of the abduction issue stoked public anger in Japan, giving prominence to victims' family members and to organizations calling for the return of the abductees. Megumi Yokota, a Japanese girl who had disappeared in 1977 at the age of 13, became a public symbol for the abductees' plight; North Korea's initial claims that she committed suicide in 1993 did not stand up to scrutiny, and her parents have expressed the belief that she may still be alive in North Korea. Given the public outcry over the abduction issue, resolving it became a top political priority for Japanese leaders in their dealings with North Korea. Shinzo Abe, a member of Prime Minister Koizumi's Cabinet and his successor as Prime Minister, gained prominence through his public advocacy for the abductees.

Shortly after the 2002 summit, North Korea allowed the five acknowledged living victims to travel to Japan with the understanding that Japan would send them back to North Korea. In order to guarantee this agreement, North Korea barred the victims' family members from traveling with them. However, after the victims' reunification with their families in Japan, the Japanese government refused to return them to North Korea and also demanded repatriation for the victims' families still residing in North Korea.

In May 2004, Prime Minister Koizumi returned to North Korea in order to negotiate the release of the families of the abductees. Following this visit, five children of returned abductees were allowed to leave North Korea for Japan. In November 2004, North Korea repatriated what it said were the remains of Megumi Yokota to Japan; however, subsequent DNA tests raised questions in Japan about the true identity of the remains, and about whether North Korea would be willing to settle remaining issues related to the abductions in good faith. North Korea, on the other hand, subsequently described the abduction issue as "solved" and insisted that Japan take steps to normalize relations and provide compensation for the colonial era.

Not long after the first Koizumi-Kim summit was held in 2002, the U.S. accused North Korea of clandestinely developing a uranium enrichment program in violation of the Agreed Framework. KEDO subsequently halted energy shipments to North Korea. In response, North Korea declared the 1994 agreement nullified, withdrew from the Nuclear Non-Proliferation Treaty, and began to reprocess plutonium. Six Party Talks to address the new nuclear crisis, involving the U.S., China, Russia, Japan, and the two Koreas, began in August 2003. Japan sought to address the abduction issue as well as the nuclear issue through these talks, leading at times to tensions with other participants.

The first several years of the talks did not lead to any progress on the abduction issue, or to any concrete actions limiting North Korea's nuclear programs. After the DPRK tested a nuclear device on October 9, 2006, Japan imposed sanctions banning all North Korean imports and prohibiting the Mangyongbong-92 ferry from entering the country. (These unilateral sanctions went beyond the scope of those imposed by the United Nations Security Council following the nuclear test, or by subsequent Security Council resolutions related to North Korea.)

Japan's unilateral decision to sanction North Korea beyond the U.N. mandate demonstrates is extreme displeasure with North Korea as well as betraying Japan's insecurity over its ability to protect itself from external aggression. Having been the only victim of a nuclear attack, Japan is understandably concerned that a hostile country, in close proximity, has defied agreements and pursued nuclear weapons.

Japan also has limited ability to respond by other means given that a third party primarily governs its ~~CSA~~ defense. The U.S. has tried to reassure Japan and other allies in the region by introducing a massive influx of military might into the region. Japan, nonetheless does not have true sovereignty to make decisions about its own protection.

As the Six Party Talks process began to gain momentum in early 2007, the negotiators established a bilateral "Working Group on the Normalization of Japan-DPRK Relations" to address the abductions and the issue of Japanese reparations for colonial rule. In several meetings held through this forum, North Korea indicated a willingness to change its previous position that it had fully investigated and settled the abduction issue, but ultimately backed away from reaching a new agreement. As other Six Party Talks members began delivering heavy fuel oil to North Korea as part of the negotiation process, Japan expressed an unwillingness to contribute energy assistance until the abduction issue had been satisfactorily resolved. In October 2008, as part of an effort to revive the now-faltering talks, the U.S. agreed to remove Pyongyang from its list of State Sponsors of Terror; some Japanese officials and family members of abductees strongly opposed the move, tying North Korea's support for terrorism with the abduction issue.

While North Korea technically fits the description as a state sponsor of terror, its involvement in terrorist activities mostly date back to the 70s and 80s. The Bush (Jr.) administration changed the designation in the hopes it could revive negotiations with North Korea by providing it with a clean slate moving forward. Japan wanted the designation to remain in order to provide it with leverage in resolving the ancillary abductee issues.

In 2009, North Korea's relations with Japan deteriorated significantly. With the Six Party Talks having faltered over the terms of a verification agreement, North Korea tested several ballistic missiles, including a three-stage Unha-2 space launch vehicle, followed by a second nuclear test. The Japanese government responded by extending its existing sanctions and adopting new measures, instituting a blanket ban on all exports to the DPRK.

Facing restrictions on contact and trade with North Korea, financial difficulties, and declining support among Zainichi Koreans, Chongryon has become a diminished force in recent years, with membership falling from 500,000 at the organization's peak to about 150,000 today. By 2009, Chongryon had closed most of its credit unions and two-thirds of its schools, despite reported subsidies to these schools from the government of North Korea. By June, 2012,

74

a Japanese court ordered Chongryon to auction off its headquarters building in Tokyo in order to pay its outstanding debts; Chongryon lost ownership of its headquarters in 2015, although it has continued to lease space in the building. In March 2015, Japanese police raided the home of Chrongryon chairman Ho Jong Man on suspicion of illegally importing North Korean mushrooms into Japan, and later arrested four people, including Ho's son, in connection with the probe.

Relations between North Korea and Japan remained cold for the first two years after Kim Jong Un assumed power. Tokyo condemned North Korea's April 2012 satellite launch, timed to commemorate the 100th birthday of Kim Il Sung. In August 2012, the Japanese and DPRK Red Cross Societies met in China, nominally to discuss the repatriation of the remains of Japanese soldiers and personnel who died in Korea during World War II. Japan suspended planned follow-up to these talks after a second North Korean satellite launch in December 2012. After North Korea's third nuclear test in February 2013, Japan further expanded its unilateral sanctions regime. The following month, Japan co-sponsored with the EU a UN Human Rights Council resolution that established a Commission of Inquiry to investigate North Korean human rights abuses, including a provision requiring the Commission to look into North Korea's abductions of foreign nationals.

Even with tensions high, however, periodic back-channel diplomacy between Tokyo and Pyongyang continued to take place, with Isao Iijima, a top advisor to Japanese Prime Minister Shinzo Abe meeting secretively with North Koreans in Pyongyang and China in May and October 2013. In March 2014, Japan-DPRK Red Cross talks on the repatriation of war remains resumed in China. Shortly after that round of talks, the parents of Megumi Yokota met with Megumi's daughter, Kim Eun-gyong, in Ulan Bator, Mongolia. In May, Japan and North Korea resumed formal diplomatic talks in Stockholm, Sweden, with a follow-up meeting held in Beijing two months later. Shortly after the second meeting, Pyongyang announced that it would reopen its investigations into the abductions cases, while Tokyo loosened sanctions by lifting some travel bans, relaxing restrictions on remittances, and allowing port calls by North Korean ships for "humanitarian" purposes. Prime Minister Abe, who had focused heavily on the abduction issue earlier in his career, said that he would aim for a "complete resolution" of the abduction issue.

There was little initial progress in North Korea's "reinvestigation" of the abduction issue, with an October 2014 Japanese Foreign Ministry delegation to Pyongyang achieving no new breakthroughs. Amidst this stalled process, Japan co-sponsored a UN General Assembly resolution condemning North Korea's violations of human rights, which included language specifically about the abduction issue and encouraged the UN Security Council to consider referring North Korea to the International Criminal Court. In response to the resolution, North Korea's National Defense Commission stated that if Japan *"continues behaving as now, it will disappear from the world map for good, not just remaining a near yet distant country."*

Relations currently are at a standstill, as Japan continues to wait for an abduction report, and North Korea articulates the need for Japan to apologize and pay reparations for its colonial actions before negotiations can move forward. During informal talks with North Korea in March 2015, Japan indicated that it would re-impose the sanctions that had been suspended if progress on the abduction issue was not made. Chief Cabinet Secretary Yoshihide Suga subsequently announced a July 4 deadline for a North Korean report on the abduction issue, with other members of the Japanese government indicating willingness to both expand sanctions and to continue dialogue with North Korea after the deadline. North Korea has linked further talks to Japan's recent probe into illicit imports by the Chongryon leadership, warning that "under such situation it is hard to hold DPRK-Japanese inter-governmental dialogue."

The Trump administration has changed the status of North Korea back to that of a state sponsor of terrorism. North Korea has successfully launched ICBM missiles assumed to be capable of hitting the continental United States. As both a veiled threat and assurance to the other nations in the region, North Korea has declared that only the United States need fear a nuclear attack provided other countries do not align themselves with the America The U.S. and Japan maintain a very close relationship.

77

South Korea

North and South Korea share a common desire for reunification. They differ in how that unification should occur and which government should rule. As with the East and West division in Germany, the people are one unit, artificially divided by others and governed by divergent political beliefs. As with the division in Germany, family units were often broken apart by bifurcation of the country.

According to Kelly, Robert, 2013, *the Korean division is now approaching its eighth decade. South Korea, and North Korea, remain locked in a surprisingly persistent cold war struggle. Although most observers would conclude that North Korea has lost the competition by almost any metric, most obviously, economic performance, the North soldiers on. Relations between the two are poor, erratic, and prone to crisis. The demilitarized zone dividing them remains, ironically, the most militarized place on earth with roughly two million soldiers and tens of thousands of tanks, rockets, and artillery within 75 miles on either side.*

This brief will summarize North Korea's survival efforts and antagonism of South Korea since the conclusion of the Cold War, the decisive turning point against the North in the inter-Korean competition. Broadly I will argue that inter-Korean relations could improve the ideological divisions are mostly moot with the passing of communism and North Korea desperately needs external assistance. However, the Kim dynasty of Pyongyang, the family leadership caste, has a vested interest in avoiding reconciliation; it would throw their brutal behavior

78

into high relief and raise the possibility of unification which likely means the absorption of North Korea. China, North Korea's patron, also has little interest in reconciliation. Hence the stalemate and cycle of provocation continues.

The Cold War divided several nations into competing states Korea, Germany, Vietnam, China, and Yemen. In each case, a broad sense of underlying national-cultural unity was maintained in the face of an artificial political separation. Unification was to take place at some point in the future. The unstated assumption was that one political model would out-race the other, highlighting the other's obsolescence and triggering unification. This roughly occurred in Germany and Vietnam. By the end of their internal competitions, it was increasingly clear that the loser had no popular legitimacy and no further viability as a separate national state. This too is the case in Korea. It is the root of the widespread expectation that North Korea will one-day collapse and that the South will extend its jurisdiction over the entire peninsula. Conversely, no one plausibly believes that Northern-led unification is a possibility any longer. Even North Korea itself admits that South Korea has outperformed it economically. The Korean race is all but over. Pyongyang's primary interest today is to forestall unification to protect the North Korean elite deeply implicated in human rights abuses and corruption despite pro-forma declarations that it still seeks unity.

The cause is South Korea's tremendous economic performance. With just fifty million people, it is today

Key

the world's thirteenth largest economy and member of the G-20. It overcame crushing, third-world levels of poverty in the 1950s. For a brief period, until the late 1960s, North Korea did outgrow South Korea, and Northern-led unification seemed possible after the US defeat in Vietnam. The North's long-serving first leader, Kim Il-Sung, even asked at the Soviet Union and China at the time for support for a second unification war. But all such talk faded by the 1980s. North Korea had begun to stagnate as its Soviet sponsor was doing. South Korea began to seriously pull-away, questioning for the first time the legitimacy of North Korea's very existence. The North's existence as a communist state was premised ideologically on its ability to deliver better, or at least, fairer, economic growth than the South. By the 1980s this was clearly untrue, and the North Korean population increasingly knew that too. So desperate was the North to block the 1988 Seoul Olympics, which would demonstrate this Southern superiority to the world, that it blew up a South Korean airliner in 1987.

North Korean agents hid a bomb on Korean Airlines flight 858, traveling from Baghdad to Seoul killing all onboard. The bombing was intended to destabilize the South Korean government as well as to scare off participants during the 1988 Seoul Olympics. There is substantial concern that North Korea will try to disrupt the Pyeongchang, South Korea Olympics, to be held in 2018.

The disappearance of the Soviet Union worsened the economic stagnation; North Korea was far more dependent on Soviet credit and concessionary fuel than outsiders realized. The crisis of the 1990s worsened with the death of Kim Il-Sung in 1994 and transfer of leadership to his untested son, Kim Jong-Il. Jong-Il, fearful of his position, elevated the North Korean People's Army to a unique role (the military first policy). The military of the North has since systematically stripped resources from the civilian economy and the onset of a series of bad harvests in turn generated an unprecedented famine. Estimates range as high as three million deaths, which would exceed 10% of the population.

The combined impact of these overlapping crises and South Korea's clear economic superiority was to throw the North into a permanent legitimacy crisis. People began to wonder why did North Korea even exist anymore, when a wealthy, healthy, prosperous Korean alternative existed right next door. The long-standing ideological reason for the North's existence, the Cold War, was now gone; Germany, Korea's most obvious parallel of cold war division, was unified. Like East Germany, North Korea was poorer, less educated, growing more slowly, corrupt, badly administered, and Orwellian. East Germany's demise was welcomed, as would be North Korea's. Predictions were common in the 1990s that the North would implode soon. In South Korea, a policy of détente, the Sunshine Policy, was adopted in the late 1990s to coax collapsing North Korea into the global post-cold war system. As the post-cold war era matured, North Korea was increasingly seen as a dangerous, bizarre anachronism, forcing Pyongyang into ever more complex contortions to justify its own continuing existence.

The North's response to its dramatic reversal of fortune in the 1990s was to accelerate its nuclear program and increasingly turn regime ideology from Marxism to racist nationalism and a theocratic cultism of the Kim family.

Despite the North's formal commitment to unification with the South, the regime likely does not want unity. North Korea is arguably the world's worst human rights abusers. It is likely that Korean unification would lead to widespread calls for the prosecution of the Pyongyang elite. The top military brass, high officials in the communist party, and loyalists of the Kim family are all broadly complicit in the network of gulags, torture, Orwellian surveillance, and indoctrination for which North Korea is notorious. Unification scenarios inevitably require the loosening of the North's police state in exchange for Southern assistance. It is simply impossible to imagine South Korea, an established democracy, becoming more authoritarian to accommodate Pyongyang, and the North needs Southern assistance, not vice versa. As a result, any meaningful federation would impact one-party rule in the North, eventually exposing the murderous Pyongyang network to outside scrutiny that would heighten pressure for serious political change. The risks to the Kim elite of unity are enormous, including facing the hangman's noose in united Korea, but they are ideologically trapped into public support for unity.

The North must continually manufacture conflicts to justify its increasingly inexplicable existence, and it must re-invent itself ideologically now that

communism is no longer popular. This was the
purpose behind events such as the Cheonan sinking
or the Yeongpyoeng shelling in 2010.

The Cheonan was a ship in the South Korean Navy that was sunk by a North Korean midget submarine. The incident killed 46 and injured 56 South Korean sailors onboard the Cheonan.

Yeonpyoeng is a South Korean island that fell under North Korean artillery attack in 2010. The South had been conducting artillery practice in the area and the North claimed they thought the South had fired into their area of the sea. The South responded by shelling North Korean gun positions on nearby islands. Four South Koreans ere killed and 19 were injured in the attack.

Without tension with its neighbors, North Korea
cannot explain to its own people why they are so
much poorer than their Southern cousins. North
Koreans know much more about South Korea than
ever before, because North Koreans built substantial
informal networks with Chinese during the famine.
Those trading networks, across the border, brought
in food during what North Korea calls the Arduous
March. The networks persisted afterward. Today they
bring in DVDs, flash-drives, and cell-phones that
have given North Koreans unprecedented access to
outside information.

The evolution of Northern ideology into the semi-
deification of the Kim family, serves a similar
purpose of distinguishing North from South Korea. If
the Kim monarchy carries a unique right to rule,
cloaked in myth and legend, then South Korea looks

like a shallow, illegitimate American colony by comparison. The first thing foreign visitors must do in Pyongyang when they visit is bow to gigantic statues of Kim Il-Sung and Kim Jong-Il. This submission is required of all visitors without exception.

The North's nuclear program serves to both justify North Korea's post-communist existence and to deter SK and American intervention. Pyongyang routinely asserts that the United States pursues a hostile policy toward it. The U.S. has wavered for decades on whether to pursue normalization, including recognition of North Korea's right to exist. George W. Bush famously demanded regime change by placing North Korea on its axis of evil list. South Korea also vacillates on whether to strike a long-term deal with the North for peaceful coexistence, or to push for the final collapse of North Korea and ultimate unification under the South's rule.

Nuclear weapons are a powerful deterrent. They make the costs of US and South Korean regime change in the North unbearable. A Northern nuclear strike on the Southern capital, Seoul, would be catastrophic. Nukes also enhance the prestige of the state. North Korea, a small, poor, half-country, nonetheless built these elite weapons which allows North Korea to stand tall against the South, the Americans, Japanese, and Chinese. Hence, Kim Jong-Un called the North's nuclear program the life of the nation.

A final element in the prevention of unification is Chinese support. The retraction of Soviet support in the early 1990s hit North Korea hard, accelerating the slide into the late 90s famine. Under liberal presidents in South Korea from 1998-2008, the South's assistance helped prop-up the regime. But this Sunshine Policy raised significant expectations in the South that the North would change in response to this assistance. But the expected changes would greatly threaten the very existence of North Korea, and more importantly the Pyongyang elite that benefits from the current arrangement. In the end, the Sunshine policy failed, because North Korea cannot change too much, or it will accelerate its own demise.

Pakistan

Pakistan and North Korea are both relatively poor countries, and each share a border with China. Per Capita income is roughly the same. Each country has invested substantial money in developing nuclear weapons, in theory as deterrents against attack. As with North Korea's threats to use these weapons, Pakistan has also threatened to use theirs against India in their stand-off over the disputed Kashmir region.

Physically, Pakistan is 6 times the size of North Korea and its population is 8 times as large. Its relationship with the United States has historically been tenuous, ever-changing and for the most part opportunistic on the part of both countries.

While acting as an American ally in the war in Afghanistan, and receiving aid for its help, they were aiding and abetting the main target of the war, Osama Bin Laden in a compound next to a major military base. When the top-secret stealth helicopter used in the mission crashed, Pakistan seize the wreckage and allowed China to examine it before returning it to the U.S.

According to Ramani, Samuel, 2016, On August 23, 2016, Pakistani Prime Minister Nawaz Sharif's Special Assistant on Foreign Affairs, Syed Tariq Fatemi, embarked on a four-day trip to Belarus and Kazakhstan. As Belarus and Kazakhstan are strongly opposed to nuclear proliferation, Sharif sent Fatemi to the CIS region to bolster international support for Pakistan's bid to join the Nuclear Suppliers Group (NSG), which rival India is also actively seeking to join. The Pakistani government hopes that

Islamabad's NSG accession will ease concerns about the potential distribution of Pakistani nuclear weapons to terrorist groups.

Even though China enthusiastically supports Pakistan's NSG bid, Pakistan's partnership with North Korea could derail Sharif's aspirations of joining the non-proliferation organization. Since the 1970s, Pakistan and North Korea have cooperated extensively on the development of ballistic missile and nuclear weapons technologies. Pakistan's strong alliance with China and the legacy of a major scandal linking the Pakistani military to North Korea's nuclear program have prevented Islamabad from joining UN efforts to diplomatically isolate the DPRK.

The sale of nuclear weapons or the technology to build them poses a great threat to the world. Protecting existing weapons is also a means to ensure international propping up of the existing governments since internal chaos could threaten how securely these weapons will be held and kept out of the hands of more radical factions. For example, should there be a regime change in North Korea, their weapons could fall into the hands of multiple players some of whom may themselves be radical or they may be willing to part with those weapons for financial gain, selling them to the highest bidder. Despite a possible desire amongst some for regime change, China's concerns that the world might become less stable should the North Korean regime collapse are legitimate.

While economic links between Pakistan and North Korea were established during the early 1970s, the foundations of the modern Islamabad-Pyongyang security partnership were forged during Pakistani Prime Minister Zulfikar Ali Bhutto's 1976 visit to North Korea. During his Pyongyang trip, Bhutto struck a delicate balance between U.S. and Chinese policies toward the Korean peninsula.

In line with Chinese preferences, Bhutto insisted that Korea's reunification could only occur after extensive dialogue with North Korean officials. To incorporate Washington's position, Bhutto argued that the United States and Japan needed to be involved as arbiters in the Korean reunification process. Bhutto's carefully crafted policy ensured that Pakistan was able to deepen ties with North Korea without antagonizing either of Islamabad's principal international allies.

The Pakistan-North Korea partnership expanded significantly during the 1990s, as Pakistan's pursuit of nuclear weapons and close relationship with the Taliban isolated Islamabad from the international community. The Chinese government refused to sell Pakistan M-11 missiles during this period, as Beijing attempted to normalize relations with the United States that had been strained by the deadly crackdown on the 1989 Tiananmen Square protests and subsequent Western arms embargo on China.

During the early 1990s, Pakistani Prime Minister Benazir Bhutto purchased Rodong long-range missiles from North Korea. In exchange, Pakistan supplied Pyongyang with "civilian nuclear technology" and encouraged North Korean students to study at Pakistani universities.

North Korea's rapid development of nuclear weapons and missile technology have stunned the world. They appear to be far more advanced in the process than anyone had speculated. While Pyongyang has demonstrated its ability to gain technology through cyber-attacks, most governments believe North Korea likely had help in developing its nuclear and missile programs. Suspicion quickly falls to Pakistan.

Even though Pakistan became a vital ally in the U.S. war on terror after the 9/11 attacks in 2001, Islamabad's military cooperation with North Korea continued under Pervez Musharraf's watch. In 2002, U.S. officials announced that Pakistan had exported gas centrifuges to help North Korea enrich uranium and construct a nuclear bomb. While Pakistani military officials denied their involvement in this scheme, the report's release did not trigger an official downgrade in the Islamabad-Pyongyang security partnership.

After the 2002 report's release, Musharraf prevented the United States from interrogating AQ Khan, a prominent nuclear scientist who assisted the nuclear programs of North Korea, Iran, and Libya. The Pakistani government declared Khan a "free citizen" in 2009. Senior U.S. officials emphatically opposed Pakistan's exoneration of AQ Khan, insisting that Khan remained a "serious proliferation risk."

Even though Pakistan has avoided overt military cooperation with North Korea in recent years, Islamabad remains unwilling to fully comply with UN sanctions against the DPRK. Although the last regular sea cargo route between Pakistan and North Korea was suspended in 2010, NK News recently reported that at least one major Pakistani company offers shipping service to Pyongyang.

In recent months, many Indian media outlets have released reports on Pakistani nuclear technology sales to North Korea. These allegations remain unsubstantiated. However, the presence of a North Korean consulate in Karachi and an embassy in Islamabad demonstrates that UN sanctions have not hindered diplomatic cooperation between the two.

Even though Islamabad's North Korea links have sullied Pakistan's international reputation, Pakistan has maintained its ties with North Korea for two reasons. First, Pakistan's relationship with North

Korea is a powerful display of its loyalty to China. The Chinese government has tacitly endorsed Pakistan's diplomatic support for Pyongyang during a period of near-complete international isolation.

Islamabad's nuclear technology assistance to North Korea during the late 1990s corresponded with an increase in Chinese support for Pakistan's nuclear program. Pakistan's strategic importance to China also grew. By using Pakistan as a funnel for nuclear materials entering North Korea, China could strengthen the DPRK's military capabilities without jeopardizing its intelligence sharing partnership with the United States.

China has also defended Pakistan from international criticism of Islamabad's nuclear weapons capabilities and its nonproliferation track record. If Nawaz Sharif were to unilaterally suspend Pakistan's diplomatic relationship with North Korea, China could retaliate by supporting greater international scrutiny of Pakistan's nuclear arsenal. The United States and most Western countries support India's NSG membership bid; Pakistan needs China's backing to accede to the NSG. Therefore, Sharif is unlikely to take drastic action against Pyongyang that would rankle Beijing.

Second, if Sharif suspended Pakistan's diplomatic relationship with North Korea, the Pakistani government would likely have to reopen the AQ Khan case for its break with Pyongyang to appear credible. An investigation of AQ Khan's North Korea links could discredit the Pakistani military's international reputation.

In 2011, Khan alleged that the Pakistani army had provided North Korea with nuclear materials in exchange for a $3 million bribe. If Khan's claims are confirmed by an in-depth investigation, the relationship between the Pakistani military and Sharif's government could be irreparably strained.

The AQ Khan case has been complicated by allegations that Khan was a much less significant player in Pakistan's nuclear material sales to North Korea than his public statements have implied. If an inquiry into the AQ Khan case revealed that the Pakistani military sanctioned nuclear material sales to the North Korean military without AQ Khan's facilitation, ex-President Pervez Musharraf and numerous senior Pakistani generals could be implicated. This outcome would be highly destabilizing for the Pakistani army and could increase the likelihood of a military coup against Sharif's government.

For over 40 years, Pakistan has remained one of North Korea's most consistent partners. As Pakistan wants to demonstrate to the international community that it is a rational actor that can be trusted with nuclear weapons, the future of the long-standing Islamabad-Pyongyang partnership has been called into question. Notwithstanding these concerns and Pakistan's ongoing NSG application, Sharif's political interests make a radical shift in Islamabad's North Korea policy unlikely for the foreseeable future.

Despite a prohibition against the purchasing of North Korean weapons, it is estimated that North Korea makes over a billion dollars a year by smuggling weapons to places such as Afghanistan, Pakistan, Iran, Egypt, and Syria. Weapons intercepted include rocket-propelled grenades, missile launchers, chemical weapons, spare parts, and other heavy weapons. Missile components have also been intercepted traveling from Cuba to North Korea.

Iran

If there is any country in the world which holds as much animosity towards the United States as North Korea it would be Iran. Both countries were used as pawns in the cold war. As with North Korea, Iran also sees nuclear weapons as a means to deter attack. Although the structure of the two governments are quite different (one is a theocracy and the other prohibits religion), the two countries have enough in common to cooperate with each other. Both have also survived through the burden of international sanctions and build partnerships where they can.

According to Bajoria, Jayshree, 2010, The release of U.S. diplomatic cables by WikiLeaks and North Korea's revelations about its uranium enrichment program have raised concerns about North Korea's proliferation activities, especially to Iran. "Most illicit nuclear programs depend very heavily on procurement networks, and North Korea has invested heavily in these supply networks," says Jeffrey Lewis, director of the East Asia nonproliferation program at James Martin Center for Nonproliferation Studies. "I worry that North Korea's procurement network will be open for business with other countries," he says.

One leaked cable notes that some of the shipments for ballistic missiles and components from North Korea to Iran passed through China, raising questions over China's role in proliferation, but Lewis says the evidence on whether there is any Chinese state support for these activities is murky. Lewis recommends interdiction as the best policy option to prevent a proliferation threat from Pyongyang.

"Right now, the outlook for negotiations is quite poor, so it makes a lot of sense to spend time on trying to physically restrain the North Koreans from selling things," he says.

Little is known of the precise nature of the cooperation. It is known that they were both customers of the Khan network (run by Pakistani nuclear scientist A.Q. Khan), and that they have collaborated on ballistic missiles, but there is not a lot of visibility into what kind of nuclear cooperation there might be between them. Which is not the same thing as saying it doesn't exist, just that we don't know.

Saudi Arabia has determined the risk to be too significant to ignore and has covertly purchased nuclear weapons from Pakistan and already has the necessary missiles to launch them as a countermove against Iran. So great is the threat perceived that Saudi crown Prince Muhammed Bin Salman made a clandestine trip to Israel to meet secretly with top officials. Although there are no official diplomatic channels between the two countries, they both have a common interest in defending against a nuclear armed Iran. The Saudis also needed to ensure the Israeli's would accept their obtaining nuclear weapons without viewing them as a threat to Israel itself.

The new evidence that North Korea has a uranium enrichment facility raise concerns that it might be helping Iran enrich uranium or that Iran might be helping North Korea. The centrifuge design that the North Koreans got from Pakistan is very similar to the one that the Iranians got, and so just as the two countries' ballistic programs are based on common designs and can involve common work, it can easily be imagined the same thing for the centrifuge program. The other thing that's important is that the most illicit nuclear programs depend heavily on procurement networks, and there's no reason to think that North Korea might not use Iran's procurement network or vice versa. There's a lot of opportunity for collaboration, just so far, we haven't found the evidence of it yet.

The UN Security Council released a report saying North Korea continues "to market and export its nuclear and ballistic technology to certain other states." The report expressed concerns about Pyongyang's cooperation with Iran, Syria, and Burma.

In 2011 the United States intercepted a ship bound for Burma. It was suspected of carrying missiles and missile technology from North Korea. Rather than allowing itself to be boarded, the ship turned around and returned to North Korea. In 2017, two shipments of chemical weapons from North Korea were intercepted prior to delivery in Syria. In 2017, Iranian ships were intercepted carrying North Korean weapons to Somalia. There is no logical reason to think North Korea does not smuggle weapons and technology to and from Iran.

North Korea would sell just about anything to anyone, so in that sense they're a very large proliferation threat. The thing that has constrained the threat from North Korea in recent years has been that only Syria seemed interested in developing a North Korean-like reactor. Everybody else was going the uranium route that the Khan network had

96

promoted. But now that North Korea is in that business, it's fair to worry that North Korea's procurement network will be put at the service of other countries.

Syria actually purchased the technology and built a reactor based upon North Korean plans. In 2007, the Israeli Airforce penetrated Syrian air space at low altitude and destroyed the reactor. Syria, denied the existence of the reactor for several years following its destruction. Unlike when Israel destroyed the reactor in Iraq, there was no international condemnation because Israel did not publicize the mission and Syria was forced into a position that it needed to deny the reactor even existed.

if China did deny airspace to North Korean flights, and if China inspected a larger number of North Korean cargoes at Dalian, which is a major port in China, that would certainly reduce North Korea's ability to proliferate. There is some evidence in the past that the Iraqis and the Brazilians may also have collaborated in part on the basis of their networks.

Centrifuges, as a route to proliferation, are essentially a collection of dual-use components. All the machinery or the materials or the actual prefabricated components that one might buy for a centrifuge are really quite similar and in some cases identical things you would buy for perfectly legitimate civilian uses. The Khan network from Pakistan included suppliers in the Netherlands, Switzerland, Spain, Turkey, South Africa. They even set up a factory in Malaysia. The technologies are quite mundane, and they're widely available. What's really threatening about a country like North Korea is that they've invested tremendous resources in putting together a supply network that is able to acquire these materials that are in components, which are supposed to be controlled, and if they can buy them for North Korea, then they can also buy them and sell them to other rogue nations and terrorist groups.

According to the U.S. diplomatic cables released by WikiLeaks, Iran has obtained ballistic missiles and missile components from North Korea, and several of these deliveries passed through China. In one instance, Washington even urged Beijing to act urgently to halt the shipment.

The West, doesn't know what to do about North Korea. It's an impossible problem, and so the natural thing to do when you're out of options is to create this kind of fictional solution and say, 'It's the

98

Chinese's fault, if the Chinese would only put pressure on the North Koreans.'

There are different levels of involvement. There are some Chinese entities that have remained involved in proliferation activities, but that's not necessarily sanctioned by the government. We also know that the North Koreans have used Chinese ports and Chinese airspace to trans-ship illicit goods. Again, that's not something that's directly the responsibility of the Chinese government. It is the responsibility of the Chinese government to adopt and enforce adequate export controls. The question of actual state support is much murkier. In the early 1980s, the Chinese provided tremendous support to the Pakistani nuclear weapons program, but it's not clear that that kind of overt support is continuing.

If China did deny airspace to North Korean flights, and if China inspected a larger number of North Korean cargoes at Dalian, which is a major port in China, that would certainly reduce North Korea's ability to proliferate. It probably wouldn't eliminate it, but nonetheless that would be the proper subject of strong U.S. efforts. It is not possible to prevent future proliferation from North Korea to Iran or to any other country without China's support.

Some top U.S. officials have recently criticized China for not doing enough on North Korea's nuclear program.

The problem is that in the West, doesn't know what to do about North Korea. It's an impossible problem, and so the natural thing to do when you're out of options is to create this kind of fictional solution and say, if the Chinese would only put pressure on the North Koreans the problem would resolve. One notable thing that you see from the WikiLeaks cables is how little the Chinese actually know about the North Korean regime, and how little influence they actually think they have. China may not be the solution we hope for.

Under the Obama administration, Iran received a deal which lifted sanctions and unfroze assets in exchange for slowing efforts towards building nuclear weapons. The agreement was met with high criticism and skepticism from people outside of the process. In reality, the deal is secret, and the details are unknown to the public, so any criticism is speculative at best. North Korea, however may view their weapons program as a negotiating tool to save its economy through the lifting of sanctions. Unfortunately for them, they may have overplayed their cards by demonstrating that they had already built nuclear weapons and a delivery system. Unlike the situation with Iran, it's difficult to agree to not build something that you have already showed the world you have built.

Cuba

Cuba is a communist country that was highly influenced by the USSR during the cold war. It is the roughly the same size as North Korea with half the population. It also has been antagonistic towards the United States and has had a history involving a standoff with the U.S. over nuclear weapons. Like North Korea, Cuba's economy was decimated when their main trade partner, the USSR collapsed.

Cuba is ideologically like North Korea. It has endured through major sanctions. The country feared invasion from the United States which was partially realized during the failed Bay of Pigs invasion. The US was fearful the USSR would base nuclear weapons in Cuba and orchestrated a naval blockade. What the U.S. did not know at the time was, those weapons were already in Cuba. Castro was insistent they be launched on Miami, New York and Washington D.C. following the Bay of Pigs fiasco, but the USSR resisted the demand.

According to Ramani, Samuel, 2016, *the Korea Times reported that senior officials from North Korea's governing Workers' Party of Korea and the Communist Party of Cuba held talks on strengthening ties between Pyongyang and Havana. This meeting followed Cuba's congratulatory rhetoric toward Kim Jong-Un after his re-election during last month's historic Workers' Party Congress. That congress was the first such-meeting since 1980.*

While relations between North Korea and Cuba have been close since the Cold War, this revelation is an embarrassing blow to the Obama administration's attempts to normalize relations with Cuba. North Korea's close ties to Cuba can be explained by a shared normative solidarity against American values and perceived American imperialism. This ideological bond is formed out of historical experience and has occasionally manifested itself in symbolically significant shipments of arms and manufactured goods. These trade linkages persist to this day, despite tightened UN sanctions and strides towards a less confrontational U.S.-Cuba relationship.

Raul Castro is 86years old and there is no heir apparent to the future leadership of Cuba. Now that diplomatic relations between Cuba and the U.S. have resumed, it can be expected that the younger generation of Cubans, who do not have an inbred compulsion to hate America, will bring change to the country. Today it is common to see young Cubans wearing clothing emblazoned with the American flag. Since diplomatic relations with the U.S. have improved, the Cuban economy has seen an upward spike. As relations improve with America it is likely that Cuba's relations with North Korea will inevitably decrease.

Over the past half-century, Cuba has been one of North Korea's most consistent international allies. This alliance has caused Havana to resist diplomatically recognizing South Korea, despite growing economic cooperation with Seoul. Cuba's firm pro-Pyongyang stance has deep ideological underpinnings, stemming from both countries shared Communist experiences. In 1960, Che Guevara visited North Korea, praising Kim Il-Sung's regime as a model for Fidel Castro's Cuba to follow.

While both regimes preserved authoritarian systems and the trappings of a planned economy, their ideological synergy did not translate into convergent governance trajectories, as Guevara predicted. North Korea wanted to avoid Cuba's dependency on Soviet weaponry following Khrushchev's retreat from confrontation during the Cuban Missile Crisis. This resulted in North Korea transitioning toward a military-first policy, to the detriment of the country's economic development. Meanwhile, despite visiting North Korea in 1986, Fidel Castro avoided creating a cult of personality resembling Pyongyang's, as he felt that statues erected in his honor were incompatible with the Soviet Marxist-Leninist principles that he adhered to.

Panama's interception of a North Korean ship in 2013 containing Cuban arms concealed under bags of sugar represented the most significant Havana-Pyongyang commercial linkage since the 1980s.

Despite Cuban attempts to downplay the controversy, Panama's foreign minister regarded this action as just part of a much larger Cuba-North Korea arms deal. U.S. Ambassador to the United Nations, Samantha Power, also condemned Cuba for violating international sanctions.

While it may be just a coincidence, Kim Jong Un executed the North Korean Ambassador to Cuba in 2013, shortly after this event in Panama.

The U.S.-Cuba normalization has thus far done little to shake Cuba's close ties with North Korea. In March 2015, Cuban Foreign Minister Bruno Rodriguez declared that Cuba maintained solidarity with the North Korean regime, despite Pyongyang's increased international isolation. Rodriguez justified his stance on the grounds that Cuban foreign policy is based on upholding just principles and resisting Western interference into the internal affairs of countries.

While leading North Korea expert Andrei Lankov interpreted these statements as proof that Cuba's criticisms of U.S. imperialism would continue unabated despite the normalization, some NK News analysts have contended that Cuba's show of support for North Korea may be more rhetorical than substantive. Cuba is mentioned only sporadically by the North Korean state media, and in a limited range of contexts.

Even if the extent of the relationship has been periodically exaggerated, Cuba's September 2015 and May 2016 reaffirmations of an alliance with

North Korea suggest that the ideological partnership remains alive and well. South Korean Foreign Minister Yun Byung-Se's visit to Cuba for the Association of Caribbean States summit and Seoul's open calls for normalization with Cuba are unlikely to cause illicit trade between Cuba and North Korea to diminish or become more covert. This is because the symbolic significance of arms shipments and small-scale trade deals between the two countries still outweighs the economic benefits Cuba could glean from enhanced South Korean capital investments.

As Cuba improves relations with South Korea and becomes more economically dependent on trade with the South, it is likely that relations with the North will become more of a hinderance than an advantage. Cash-strapped Cuba will likely yield to the pressure of the South based upon the economic advantage it can provide Cuba.

Despite the immense international controversy resulting from Cuba's 2013 arms sales to North Korea, sporadic trade linkages between the two countries have continued largely unhindered. In January 2016, Cuba and North Korea developed a barter trade system, which officially involved transactions of sugar and railway equipment.

Barter trade is an effective way for Cuba and North Korea to evade international sanctions without depleting their hard currency reserves. Cuba's use of sugar as a medium of bilateral trade has close parallels with Burma's historical use of rice in exchange for North Korean military technology assistance. This form of trade has been vital for the

North Korean regime's survival in wake of the Soviet collapse and more inconsistent patronage from China.

While Cuba's ability to use North Korean railway equipment remains unclear, NK News reported in January that Kim Jong-un was planning to modernize the DPRK's railway networks. This development initiative could result in heavy industry production that can be bartered to Havana.

While trade in civilian goods between Cuba and North Korea appears to be on the upswing, trade in illicit arms continues to be the most symbolically potent and controversial form of bilateral trade. A 2013 Stockholm International Peace Research Institute report noted that a large number of North Korean arms brokers speak fluent Spanish. This language training demonstrates the importance of Cuba as a trade destination for the DPRK. The report notes that Cuban arms dealers are especially attractive because they can deal with North Korea with a sense of impunity. This contrasts sharply with a British arms dealer who faced prison time in 2012 for purchasing North Korean weapons.

While the 2013 incident remains the most recent confirmed incident of weapons trading between Havana and Pyongyang, recent revelations of a lost U.S. Hellfire missile turning up in Cuba have sparked fresh concerns about a revival of the long-standing arms trade.

While the Obama administration has removed Cuba from the state sponsors of terrorism list and taken a big stride toward lifting the Kennedy-era embargo on Cuba, Havana's continued cooperation with Pyongyang is an alarming blow to the normalization process. The current linkage between anti-Americanism and the Cuban Communist Party's regime security makes a shift in Havana's North Korea policy unlikely in the short-term. It remains to be seen if Castro's planned retirement in 2018 will take Cuban foreign policy in a more pragmatic direction, and allow South Korean diplomatic overtures to finally be successful.

The Kim Family

In order to understand North Korea, it is important to look at the members of the ruling dynasty. Unfortunately, this is a far more difficult task than it seems. The Kim family is shrouded in mystery which is mixed with legend, mythology, and a modicum of truth. The North Korean people are taught that the Kim family are nothing short of living Gods. Among the odder myths about the Kim family is that they do not defecate or urinate because to do so would be beneath the status of a God.

The cult of personality surrounding the Kim family requires total loyalty and subjugation to the Kim family and establishes the country as a one-man dictatorship through successive generations. The North Korean constitution incorporates the ideas of Kim Il Sung as the only guiding principle of the state and his activities as the only cultural heritage. There is a widely held belief that Kim Il Sung created the world and the Kim Jong Il controlled the weather.

After fighting a guerrilla war against the Japanese in Korea during the 1930s, Kim Il-Sung retreated to the

Soviet Union, where he joined the Red Army and rose to the rank of major. Following the Allied victory in World War II, the Soviet army occupied Korea north of the 38th parallel. Stalin installed Kim as the head of the Korean Communist Party and then of the Provisional People's Committee, which governed the Soviet-occupied area of Korea. He began to form the Korean People's Army to consolidate his power.

On Sept. 9, 1945, Kim defied a United Nations plan to hold elections throughout Korea by declaring himself Prime Minister of an independent Democratic People's Republic of Korea, or North Korea. The next month, the USSR recognized Kim's government as the legitimate authority not only in North Korea, but throughout the Korean peninsula. Kim consolidated his power by forming the Democratic Front for the Reunification of the Fatherland, a political movement in which his party took the dominant role.

Additionally, Kim promoted a cult of personality, calling himself "Dear Leader" and creating posters and statues to display his accomplishments and authority

Kim Il-Sung's power over his country and people was essentially absolute, and his word was therefore effectively law. When it came to his son's ascendancy, the elder Kim helped ensure his son's rise to power by giving him many influential and powerful positions to solidify his control.

After the Korean War, Kim Il-Sung built a cult of personality around himself, making himself the unquestioned "Great Leader" of the country. He began grooming his son for leadership early on, putting him in control of the Propaganda and Agitation department of the Workers' Party. Between 1970 and 1980, Kim Jong-Il occupied several positions of increasing power. By 1980, a personality cult began to form around him as the Great Leader's successor. He gained control of the Politburo, the Secretariat and the Military Commission, giving him control over much of the party's control apparatus. Once he gained control of the military, Kim Jong-Il became the Supreme Commander of the Korean Peoples' Army, which ensured his ascendancy.

North Korean history books state Kim Il Sung came from a long lineage of leaders. He is credited with almost single-handedly defeating the Japanese and rebuilding Korea. It was forbidden for books or newspapers to split his name between two lines, it needed to be complete on one line only. School children were taught they were fed, clothed, and cared for by the grace of Kim Il Sung. Larger elementary schools had a room dedicated only to lectures about Kim Il Sung. His birthplace, Mangyongdae-guyok became a place of pilgrimage. When Kim Il Sung died in 1994, Kim Jong Il took power, a national mourning period of 3 years was declared. The North Korean calendar was changed to coincide with the birth of Kim Il Sung (1912) as the first year, for example 2017 is actually year 106 in North Korea. The power of the Kim dynasty is absolute.

Upon his father's death, Kim Jong Il abolished the position of president, taking instead the titles of General Secretary of the Workers' Party and Chairman of the National Defense Commission. Kim Jong Il was known to the North Korean people and a mythology was created about his life as part of ensuring the cult of personality would continue after the death of his father. The people are told that Kim Jong Il was born in 1942 on Mount Paektu (a mystical site) although it is known, outside of the country that he was actually born in 1941 in the Soviet Union. The story continues that his birth was heralded by a swallow, caused winter to instantly change to spring, created a new star in the sky and a double rainbow to spontaneously appear. Propaganda said he was able to walk and talk before he was 6 months old and that his fashion sense had created a world-wide trend.

Kim Jong Il faced greater challenges than his father. When the Soviet Union collapsed, it no longer made payments to North Korea causing severe financial stress. Out of self-preservation he adopted a military first policy. After the elite, the military was to get priority over food and supplies leaving millions of poor rural citizens to die of famine.

His death was also shrouded in secrecy. It came unexpectedly and there was speculation initially that he was killed in a coup. The true story seems to be that he was angry at construction workers and while having a screaming fit suffered a heart attack. After 2 days of silence the official North Korean news reported he died peacefully, of a heart attack onboard his private train. Official national mourning was set for 100 days. After his death, the mythology continued to include stories of layers of ice cracking on Lake Chon and a major snow storm hitting his mythological birth place on Mount Paektu.

Kim Jong Un was an unlikely successor, given he was the youngest of 3 sons and that his uncle was far more well known. Kim Jong Un though, was his father's favorite, based upon a similar personality. People who questioned the succession were sent to re-education camps or punished.

Being relatively unknown, a massive campaign of propaganda began to build a legacy behind the young leader. In a show of strength, public executions for those who questioned his authority increased. In 2013, he had his uncle (and reportedly members of his uncle's immediate family, executed for undermining Kim's family personality cult. Since his rule began, 340 people were publicly executed, many in very gruesome ways.

Kim Jong-Un has had to accept that people have turned to private enterprises in order to feed themselves even though such capitalist activities are illegal. The younger generation has also become problematic because they have greater knowledge of the outside world and are less susceptible to the propaganda and personality cult activities. It is thought that the current stand-off with the United States is motivated to unify a population that is becoming more enlightened to the outside world.

Little is known about this young leader. His age is estimated to be 33-34. He is an avid basketball fan and

112

reportedly the only time he was honored on his birthday was in 2014 when Dennis Rodman sang happy birthday to him. There was no fanfare when he married, nor any public celebration when his wife gave birth.

Part of the legend of Kim Jong Un is that he has expertise in everything. It is common for him to visit everything from fish farms, to clothing factories, to military bases to share his divine guidance.

Why They Want Nuclear Weapons

Nuclear weapons combined with a delivery system are a big deterrent against enemy attack. Theoretically a country with nuclear weapons could minimize investment in other military equipment and the threat of nuclear attack would be sufficient to keep an enemy at bay.

During the cold war, the U.S. and USSR fought proxy wars throughout the world. While brutal, these wars deflected any direct conflict between the superpowers. The main reason was the risk of a direct conflict turning into a nuclear war. The risk of mutually assured destruction was a risk neither side was willing to take.

North Korea cannot win a war against the U.S. and its allies, especially without assistance from Russia and China. It can however make the consequences of war so high as to make it unacceptable. One nuclear bomb destroying San Francisco, or New York would be too high of a price to pay for the United States to rush into a war.

The U.S. has been operating with incomplete and faulty intelligence on North Korea's capabilities. North Korea appears to be a decade ahead of what was thought. The U.S. believed North Korea was using decoy weapons during parades in Pyongyang, the same way the Soviets paraded fake weaponry through Moscow, but that assumption was incorrect.

North Korea is well aware of what occurred in Iraq, Libya and Syria. Each of those countries was at various stages in developing nuclear weapons. Libya gave theirs up voluntarily, having been assured they would not be attacked. Israel destroyed Iraq and Syria's nuclear programs. Once the threat was gone, those countries came

114

under attack in attempts (2 successful) to overthrow the regimes in power.

North Korea wants to be an accepted part of the world community. Isolation has caused its people to suffer and the country to be prevented from meeting its true potential. It wants the sanctions that are crippling it to be lifted.

North Korea is aware that Iran capitulated very little in its touted deal with the United States to slow weapon development. While the details of that agreement remain secret, Iran received the benefits of a huge cash influx and the lifting of sanctions. North Korea could not base a deal off of stopping the creation of weapons because it already had them. It has been showing the world its capabilities through testing of the weapons and delivery systems to stop a preemptive strike like those that occurred in Iraq and Syria. It now must resort to extorting capitulations from the world and having sanctions lifted, preferably without losing its current capabilities. What the North can offer in return is an agreement not to share the weapons or technology with others. Selling nuclear and missile technology would be a very lucrative business for North Korea.

The regime in North Korea can only exist as long as the people allow it to exist. Kim Jong Un does not enjoy the adulation of his predecessors. People are suffering under crippling pressure. The population has been controlled by gruesome public executions and harsh punishment for those who act against the regime. It is losing control over the younger population and those gaining exposure to life outside of the country. A common enemy must be maintained to keep the population focused on an external threat as opposed to an internal one.

U.S. Vulnerabilities

The United States invests more on its military might than any other country. Its strength is not determined by sheer size of its army, but by the advanced training, technology, global resources, alliances, and dedication of its all-volunteer troops.

It does have several notable vulnerabilities. The civilian population is soft, spoiled and used to living a life of abundance. Civilians are neither physically or psychologically prepared to help defend our country should war ever reach our shores. Most of the people do not have the survival skills to cope with any disruption in food or energy supplies. Part of this vulnerability can be compensated for by the fact that many Americans own firearms.

The population is easily distracted and has a short attention span. Many are not aware of current events or basic knowledge of other countries (or even states outside of their region). While the U.S. may be engaged in major wars there is little if any direct impact on the American people as life goes on unimpeded.

Internal U.S. politics create a divided and divisive population that often hinders the government's ability to accomplish goals. Political action groups, often paid and often linked to larger groups who in the past would have been considered seditious, prevent the public from unity. The media has been exposed for biases and presenting false news, perhaps out of a desire to be the first to present a news story and skipping the vetting process, or possibly because they have become politicized themselves. It is difficult for citizens who wish to be informed to find trustworthy news sources unless they look outside the U.S. media.

The United States remains one of the wealthiest countries in the world, but it has become burdened with an enormous national debt. Some of that debt is held by foreign countries that could severely impact the economy of the United States should they become displeased with U.S. policy and choose to sell their treasury bonds. The majority of the national debt has been "purchased" by Social Security and Medicare. Failure of the U.S. government to pay back this debt will result in a collapse of the social service system leaving many people destitute. Any sustained war would only increase the amount of national debt.

The American political system makes it difficult to adopt long term strategic plans. Presidents can only serve a maximum of 8 years and are often usurped by the opposing political party which dismantles plans of the prior administration and takes the country in a new direction. While countries like China can effectively plan fifty years in advance, it is far more difficult for America to do the same. This extends to war. Wars started under one administration may be defunded under the next. Despite the loss of lives, large amounts of money, resources and world opinion, these wars are ended before any tangible goals have been met, leaving places like Iraq in an unstable and vulnerable state. America's inability or unwillingness to carry through missions to completion weakens its standing amongst allies while strengthening potential enemies that know they are better off waiting out the next election cycle.

Domestic discourse is part of being American. Freedom of speech, freedom of the press, and the right to assemble are granted by the U.S. Constitution. Countries that do not have these freedoms may interpret American protests incorrectly. Protests become a custom-made propaganda machine for U.S. enemies while demoralizing American troops. They disrupt daily lives and slow the delivery of needed supplies for the population and military. Rather than unify the people civil disobedience further divides. Most recently these peaceful protests have taken a violent turn with threats against public officials, assaults on citizens and police, destruction of property, and skewed media reporting.

Military

Despite a huge budget, the Pentagon has gone beyond its allotment. It cannot account for 10 Trillion (with a T) dollars identified during a 2017 audit. The people of the United States cannot afford such a large misappropriation of tax revenue but also cannot afford to make budget cuts to the military during precarious times. Both China and Russia have made dramatic advances in their weapons technology and countering the new threats (or staying ahead) requires additional investments in research and development.

The war of terror has our military stretched by covert operations in over 100 countries plus open operations in Afghanistan, Iraq, and Syria. Resources, troops, intelligence, and support personnel are needed to manage the status quo. If America becomes locked in a war with North Korea it will be sustained, and the cost will be beyond any military action ever undertaken. The financial burden may prove to be too excessive for the economy to weather, given the national debt and misappropriated Pentagon funds.

The U.S. military cannot count on a draft to augment its numbers. The civilian population will rise up against the reintroduction of involuntary military service. If the draft were to come into effect, despite being contrary to the people's will, much of the American population is out of shape and overweight which would prove more of a burden to our professional fighting men and women than a help.

In order to recruit additional military personnel, requirements to join the armed forces have been lowered in the past year. The army is now willing to accept enlistees who have smoked marijuana in the past. The Airforce has recalled pilots who have aged out and still faces a shortage of pilots. There is a temporary hold on the removal of transgender members from the ranks. The National Guard which in the past was under state control is now federalized and members of any branch can find themselves deployed and integrated into support roles outside of their original training.

Army

Although the U.S. has many military assets which can cripple the infrastructure of North Korea fairly quickly, in the end, the U.S. Army will need to occupy the country, likely for many years. All people in North Korea are required to be in the military for 3 years, and thus have some military training. There are 1.2 million active duty North Korean troops with 10 million citizens fit for military service who can be drafted at a moment's notice. All citizens are told they must fight for their country. The chance that fighting will continue throughout an occupation is great. Despite having superior resources, the U.S. will face fierce fighting from North Koreans defending their homeland. Their sheer number will be a daunting challenge for the U.S. Army. North Korea is riddled with underground bunkers and tunnels which can provide shelter to a large amount of the population, biding time before reemerging to ambush American troops once those troop feel a region has been secured.

Nuclear Weapons

The entire world knows that North Korea definitely has nuclear weapons but knowing the exact number, if they are missile ready, or how strong the weapons are is more of a challenge. The most recent test was thought to be a hydrogen bomb which was estimated to be 10 times more powerful than the bombs dropped on Hiroshima and Nagasaki.

It is not believed that the weapons have been miniaturized to the point that they can be launched via missiles, but the intelligence analyzed may not be correct. It is certain that in time, the technology to make the weapons smaller will eventually happen, at which time, these weapons can threaten any part of the United States (or other world targets). While missile delivery is seen as the largest threat, there are several other ways these weapons can be delivered to the U.S. mainland or allies in the region.

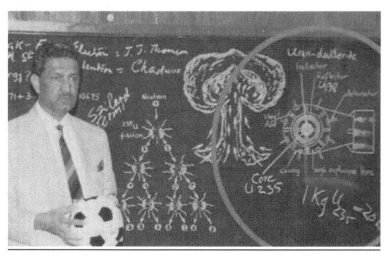

Missiles

The North Korean missile program is also shrouded in mystery. It does not appear any intelligence agency believed North Korea had functioning ICBM missiles. Those paraded around Pyongyang were thought to be a deception.

The U.S. has several land and sea based missile defense systems, the most advanced being THAAD, which has been deployed to the region. The accuracy of these defense weapons is uncertain, and North Korea would like to know as much as they can about the potential threat these missile defense systems pose to their own missiles. In 2015, North Korea sold 20 scud missiles to Yemen, two have recently been launched at Riyadh, Saudi Arabia. Both missiles were successfully shot down by the U.S. made Patriot Missile system. It is likely that North Korea played a role in these missiles being launched to assess the accuracy of U.S. missile defense. Although the Patriot system is several generations behind the capability of the THAAD system, it's successful interception of missiles in Saudi Arabia must have sent shivers across the North Korean military.

If the missile systems are effective, then North Korea does not hold the leverage it thought it did. While the THAAD system is mostly secret, opposition to its deployment by both China and Russia suggests that it is an effective system that could pose a threat to their missile systems as well.

The sea based missile defense system is called Aegis. The Aegis system is designed to intercept missiles between the boosting and re-entry stages. Due to the new threat from North Korea, Japan will be investing in the purchase of its own Aegis system from the U.S. The USS McCain and USS Fitzgerald were both mysteriously rammed by cargo vessels. U.S. Intelligence suspects that North Korea hacked into the cargo ships navigation systems causing the crashes. Both ships had Aegis ballistic missile defense equipment onboard. If North Korea does have the ability to cyber-hack into the navigation systems of cargo ships the U.S. will need to counteract this ability to preserve the integrity of the Aegis system as well as protect military and commercial shipping from this type of unorthodox attack.

The U.S. has a ground-based interceptor missile and radar system designed to detect and kill ICBM missiles. Thirty-six such interceptors are stationed in Alaska and California, and the military expects to have a total of 44 in place by the end of 2017. This is a final line of defense for the United States.

Nullifying North Korea's missile capabilities does not eradicate the nuclear threat, it just makes delivery more challenging.

Prop Planes

North Korea has a fleet of 300 old biplanes which can fly as slow as 30 miles per hour. These planes fly so slowly that modern radar cannot track them. While these planes lack the range to reach the United States, they can carry a nuclear cargo to be detonated over Japan, South Korea or even as far away as Guam with little or no warning whatsoever.

Prop planes could also be used to deliver biological or chemical weapons over a heavily populated city without warning.

Cargo Ships

North Korea has 122 cargo ships. They have been caught several times smuggling weapons throughout the world. UN sanctions allows ships to be intercepted and boarded under specific conditions. The United States is seeking greater UN approval to intercept and inspect all North Korean vessels.

In order to circumvent UN sanctions, some of these ships have been renamed; with front companies in Hong Kong assuming ownership of these North Korean ships. 50 of these cargo ships are in the process of being reflagged to the flag of Tanzania, again in hopes of avoiding international sanction.

As a rogue nation that does not follow international laws, North Korea could bypass the official reflagging and disguise their ships to appear to be from any other country in the world, without consequence.

North Korea could potentially deliver nuclear weapons via cargo ships. Ostensibly on a trade mission with its ally, Cuba, North Korea could conduct a kamikaze nuclear attack on Miami, New Orleans, and Houston. Each of those cities has strategic importance to the survival of the United States.

The ships could take a longer route to avoid possibility of having their hidden cargo discovered while traveling through the Panama Canal, or use the Panama

Canal as a back-up target. Destroying the canal would hugely impact U.S. military and commercial shipping, causing significant physical, psychological, and strategic damage.

North Korea allowed millions of people to starve to death for the sake of preserving the regime, suicide missions (known or unknown to the crew) are certainly within the realm of possibility. Between the ability to commandeer ship navigation systems to crash into targets and disguising ownership of ships to transport weapons more easily, including nuclear weapons; cargo ships pose a far greater threat than in the past.

Submarines

North Korea's hidden submarine threat is another worry as the regime warns it's ready for war. The North is known to have 70 submarines, but it suspected of having more. At 70, it has the second largest submarine fleet in the world, only surpassed by the United States. The quality of those submarines may be low in comparison to other navies but the quantity of submarines and the experience of their sailors which averages 10 years, is still a threat.

The chilling thought of North Korea's fully submersible submarines firing a nuclear ballistic missile is a real possibility. There are fears the North Korean dictator is adapting his fleet of subs, so they can fire warheads amid heightened tensions with the West. Satellite images taken by U.S. satellites show what appear to be missile tubes being installed on some of these vessels. It is possible though, that these tubes are decoys created to frighten or confuse. Submarine based launches require a great deal of skill and knowledge that North Korea does not likely have at this time. In time they will develop this capability which is strategically important in providing a second trike option should ground based missiles be destroyed.

Kim Jong-Un is increasing his underwater military capabilities and may even have plans in place to launch nuclear missiles from a submarine. The North has stolen plans for more advanced submarines from South Korea and is said to be in the process of mass-producing them at this time.

The submarine threat adds to growing fears in the region as North Korean leader Kim Jong Un's nuclear weapons ambitions show no signs of slowing.

North Korean subs have already proven to be elusive. Recently, 50 vessels, which account for 70 per cent of Pyongyang's known submarines, disappeared off radar sparking panic in South Korea and Japan in the wake of a tense stand-off with South Korea. This is very worrisome because they may very well carry nuclear weapons in the future.

It is believed that dictator Kim Jong-Un's nuclear submarine system is inspired by the Golf-class submarines used by the Soviet Union before the fall of the Iron Curtain.

Japanese Prime Minister Shinzo Abe said he feared Kim Jong-Un has a capability to fire missiles tipped with sarin; the same deadly gas used to kill 87 Syrian civilians in a horrifying gas attack in 2017. There is a strong possibility that North Korea already has a capability to deliver missiles with sarin as their payload.

According to Daniels, Jeff, 2017 *the nuclear attack threat from a North Korean submarine is one of the nightmare scenarios facing Japan and South Korea.*

Pyongyang has made major advances in weapons in recent years and shown a willingness to use its submarines for offensive military actions.

2017 marked the seventh anniversary of the sinking of South Korea's Cheonan navy ship by a North Korean submarine torpedo attack. That aggression killed 46 sailors and wasn't the first time the reclusive North had made incursions into South Korean waters.

The U.S. has deployed 3 carrier groups to the region. Not surprisingly, North Korea decried the deployment of the American carrier task forces. North Korea stated, if the U.S. dares opt for a military action the DPRK is ready to react to any mode of war desired by the U.S.

Experts believe North Korea's navy has around 70 submarines in its fleet, although only a handful today are believed to be capable of firing submarine-

launched ballistic missiles or so-called SLBMs. And while North Korea does not yet appear to have a functional, operational submarine-launched nuclear capability they are testing submarine missiles that could someday carry a nuclear warhead.

North Korean media showed off video of a so-called KN-11 submarine missile being launched from eastern coastal waters. The submarine-launched missile flew about 310 miles toward Japan. The test set a new distance record for Pyongyang's SLBM program, and experts suggest the ballistic missile has the capability to travel more than 600 miles.

Klingner, a former CIA deputy division chief for Korea, explained that the THAAD anti-missile system deployed last month by the U.S. in South Korea is focused on identifying missile threats from the North. As a result, a submarine missile from the North Korean navy could be launched behind radar and evade defense systems.

Similarly, missiles fired by North Korean submarines off the east coast of Japan might be able to dodge detection from Japan's Patriot anti-missile system by launching from behind radar.

Joint U.S.-South Korea military exercises in 2017 included drills on destroying the North's submarines.

Klingner said some people have been dismissive of the Pyongyang submarine threat by maintaining that the North's vessels are "old and noisy." The noise comes from the submarine's diesel-powered engines.

Yet in 2015 South Korean defense officials reported a sudden disappearance of around 50 of the North's submarines.

"We didn't know where they were at the time," said Klingner. "One would hope that we would keep very close tabs on those that could launch the SLBM."

Advances in North Korea's land-based weapons development have been helped by its submarine program.

As an example, Pyongyang in February showed off a new medium- to long-range ballistic missile that is capable of carrying a nuclear warhead and uses solid-fuel technology. The land-based ballistic missile is believed to use the same technology of the KN-11 solid-fuel submarine missiles.

Solid fuel offers significant advantages over liquid-fuel rockets because it makes the missile easier to hide, requires less support and allows for faster launches.

Even without missile capability, North Korea's submarines could pose a significant threat. Acting in concert, they could carry out a sustained torpedo attack on one of the American aircraft carriers in the region. During World War 2, the Japanese battleship Yamato was the heaviest and most armored battleship ever constructed. It was thought to be unsinkable, but a sustained American attack focusing all attacks on one side of the ship, forced it to capsize and sink. A similar strategy against an aircraft carrier, using all available North Korean subs could produce a similar result.

A submarine does not need to be able to launch a missile in order to be a nuclear threat. The submarine itself could serve as the delivery system. A nuclear weapon could be carried on the submarine into San Francisco Bay or Long Beach Harbor; surface and detonate the weapon in a kamikaze inspired mission. There is an ongoing hunt for North Korean submarines along the Canadian and American west coasts.

Bio Weapons

North Korea is known to have biological weapons and intelligence agencies report that they are intensifying production. Bio weapon development is more difficult to locate than missile sites or nuclear testing grounds since they can be created and stored in smaller structures that could resemble any kind of building. Open bombing of biological weapons sites comes with a greater risk that the contagions will be widely dispersed and as such destruction of these sites requires special care by experts.

In December 2017, a defectors from the North was determined to have had exposure to Anthrax.

North Korea is known to have chemical weapons. The development of these weapons began in 1954. North Korea received aid from China and the USSR to develop its chemical industry which operated side by side with the development of chemical weapons. It is thought that North Korea has a stockpile of 5000 tons of chemical weapons including mustard gas, sarin and nerve agents. North Korean ships have been intercepted delivering chemical weapons to Syria.

Of the known chemical and biological weapons sites, all are close to the Russian or Chinese borders. Should these sites succumb to U.S. bombing raids it is highly likely that the fallout would reach both of those border countries raising the threat of the conflict expanding.

132

Cyber-attacks

It is difficult to understand how a backward and isolated country such as North Korea has developed such significant abilities with cyber warfare. The North has nonetheless resorted to cyber-attacks against its adversaries with increasing scale and capacity. This is worrisome because advanced cyber warfare capabilities could increase North Korea's advantage and allow it to escalate a crisis using alternative means. South Korean banks and broadcasting systems are a frequent target of attacks. North Korea has 6000 government employed hackers who are both persistent and improving in their skill set.

In 2016 North Korean hackers attempted to steal One billion dollars from the account of the Bangladesh Central Bank held at the New York Federal Bank. The attack would have been successful had a spelling error not been caught during the transfer process. The hackers still managed to steal 81 million dollars in that attack.

In 2017 North Korean hackers attempted a ransomware attack. The attack failed to generate much cash but caused hundreds of thousands of computers worldwide to crash, including that of Britain's National Health Service.

During the Obama administration, North Korea was blamed for hacking into the Sony Corporations computer system and retaliated by shutting down the North Korean internet. The United States thought it was being strong and bold, but its weaknesses were exposed. The Sony attack was likely conducted by a disgruntled worker and not North Korea. In blaming North Korea for the attack, America showed that it did not have sufficient ability to identify where an attack was coming from and thus emboldening North Korea to pursue future attacks. By retaliating, the United States had to go through China's computers, which supply North Korea with the internet. In doing so, both China and North Korea were able to learn how the U.S. accomplishes cyber-warfare, potentially allowing them to counteract it in the future. Given that the Sony hack was not of national security interest, it made little sense to expose American cyber methods and may hinder its use on more important matters in the future.

Keystone American Cities

The United States has many large cities. Several of those cities have more strategic value than others. If America's enemies were to successfully destroy just 6 cities the rest of the country would be crippled in the process. This is a vulnerability known to the American government and its enemies alike.

New York City is the financial hub for the United States and much of the world. Major world banks are headquartered in New York as is the New York Stock

Exchange. It is the headquarters for many major companies. It plays a large role in the production of national news, television, communications, and transportation. The port is important in the transportation of goods in and out of the northeastern United States. This city alone accounts for 8.6% of the U.S. Gross Domestic Product (GDP) The city's GDP is greater than that of Australia. A nuclear attack on this city would cripple trade, collapse financial markets, hinder communication systems, and break supply routes.

Washington D.C. is the political capital of the United States and houses the President, Congress, all Government Departments, and the Pentagon. Washington's GDP is greater than that of Sweden. The destruction of this city would cause a breakdown in leadership, federal subsidies to states and cities to stop, social security payments and federal employee payments, including the military, to cease. The loss of military command structure would cause chaos for the armed forces. Everything from roads to schools would be impacted throughout the country.

Chicago is a broadcasting center. It is home to the Chicago Mercantile Exchange, Chicago Stock Exchange, and is an important transportation hub for airplanes, railroads, and shipping. Chicago is a major world financial center. The City of Chicago alone has a GDP greater than Indonesia. Chicago has become one of the most important business centers in the world. The destruction of this city would cause major disruptions in food distribution throughout the country and disrupt national communication systems. It would seriously impact financial institutions around the world.

Houston is one of the global capitals of energy and energy services. It is home to the Johnson Space Center and 20 Fortune 500 companies. It's GDP is greater than that of Argentina. The city is responsible for much of the fuel refining in the country and is a major transportation center. Destruction of this city would disrupt shipping, trucking and rail transportation for goods and materials but most significantly the production and delivery of fuel.

Miami has the largest concentration of international banks in the United States. It is the headquarters for the Latin operations for more than 1400 multinational corporations. Miami's GDP is higher than South Africa. Miami is a major television production center and the most important city in the U.S. for Spanish language media. Miami/Fort Lauderdale account the second largest cargo shipping port on the East Coast (after New York/New Jersey). It is home the largest passenger port in the world. Miami is home to the Southern Naval Command. The destruction of this city would impact communication and disrupt export/imports primarily to and from Latin America.

Los Angeles is America's second largest city by population and combined with Long Beach has a cargo shipping capacity that is 3 times larger than New York/New Jersey. Its GDP is greater than that of Turkey. Los Angeles is the west coast hub for national news and communication. Los Angeles is a center for fuel production, refinement, and distribution. Its extensive highways provide transportation for food from the extensive growing regions that surround the city and beyond. Destruction of this city would cripple food supplies, transportation, communication, and fuel resources for the entire west coast of the United States.

Knowing the vulnerability of these cities, the U.S. government has additional protections in place for these cities including radiation detection, extensive surveillance, and counter-terrorism units. If enemy combatants are willing to sacrifice their lives though, stopping an attack becomes immensely more difficult.

Escalation to Russia and China

If the United States was to take unilateral action against North Korea it would need to be rapid and overwhelming. Unfortunately, rapid and overwhelming will come with significant consequences. North Korea has strategically placed its Nuclear, Biological, Chemical, and Missile development facilities close to the Chinese and Russian borders. A massive attack on these facilities will disperse radioactive, chemical, and biological weapons throughout the region, including harming Russian and Chinese citizens.

Although this would be a consequence of North Korean weapons being destroyed and not a planned attack on China or Russia, both countries would likely feel a need to retaliate.

EMP

EMP stands for Electro-Magnetic Pulse weapons. China, Russia, and the United States are thought to have true EMP weapons. Much of what the public thinks they know about these weapons is based upon fiction and popular culture (T.V., Movies etc.).

Once North Korea demonstrated that it has nuclear capability, the American news began reporting that the greatest threat to America would be if North Korea detonated a nuclear weapon high in our atmosphere. The narrative suggests that such an explosion would cripple the nations electric grid and kill millions of people within a week.

This narrative is an exaggeration at best and a fallacy at worst. In almost any scenario the impact would be minimal at best. It would not likely impact vehicles, cell phones, airplanes or any electronic equipment that is off or secured with a surge protector. It is unlikely to permanently impact the grid or delivery system.

The narrative may be a disinformation campaign designed to make North Korea think they could cause more damage with a high-altitude explosion rather than a direct hit on an American city. The United States does not want to appear to be the aggressor and, as always, wants it to appear any attack is a response to an attack by another country. In the case of North Korea, the cost of allowing them to attack first is too great, but if they exploded a nuclear weapon high in the atmosphere above the U.S., world opinion would support America to respond, while the U.S. suffers far less damage than would occur if the same bomb hit Los Angeles.

While it is true the U.S. has some vulnerabilities, it is important to note the U.S. government is aware of these vulnerabilities and are doing whatever possible to secure the country.

North Korea Vulnerabilities

North Korea believes it knows everything there is to know about America's capabilities but does not realize U.S. military weapons are decades ahead of what is known to the public. The U.S. did not acknowledge having stealth planes until 1989 but development began in the late 60's. In part the secrecy is kept so China and Russia will not develop weapons based upon U.S. concepts. However, when China and Russia demonstrated that they had hyper-sonic propulsion technology, the U.S. quickly responded by launching its own craft from Greenland, which created a sonic boom heard on both sides of the Atlantic.

When stealth helicopters were needed for the raid on Bin Laden's compound in Pakistan, they were top secret, but they already existed and were available for the mission.

While North Koreas technology is impressive based upon the speed of development and ability to proceed despite sanctions, U.S. technology is far more advanced.

Sanctions are having an effect on North Korea, albeit predominantly amongst the poor. As mass starvation and malnutrition increase so will disease that could create an epidemic and impact all, rich and poor.

Rich and Poor

The regime in North Korea is failing to provide for its people, who eventually will either die or band together to overthrow the government. The supposed Stalinist state actually has more class distinctions based upon songbun than any other society. It is not a classless society proposed by Stalinism. A few elites ruling in luxury surrounded by a large population of starving peasants is a classic recipe for revolution.

As the population poses a threat to the regime, the threat can be measured by an increase in government crackdowns and an increase in public executions. If trained and fed, the internal population will revolt against this regime as they did throughout eastern Europe after the collapse of the USSR.

News from Outside

The population is becoming more aware of the outside world. A dramatic increase in outside news will cause the North Koreans to further question the myths they have been told about their country and the Kim regime.

A large part of keeping the regime in power is that the people have only known what the government has told them. As alternate news becomes available, people will begin to pull at the threads of the myths and discover that they have been duped into supporting a despot regime.

Too Much Information

The United States has difficulty assessing information from North Korea. The media is entirely controlled by the government and is used mainly for propaganda. The few visitors to North Korea are not free to explore outside of a highly controlled and orchestrated tour. Much of the information gathered about North Korea comes from satellite images and speculations based upon the frequency of public appearances by Kim Jong Un and a cursory assessment of his health based upon his appearance. The U.S. is challenged by having too little information available about North Korea.

American media and internet are the exact antithesis of North Korea. Information flows freely (or appears to). The sheer volume of information combined with oppositional narratives must overwhelm North Korea's ability to accurately analyze intelligence.

The American media is easily deceived and manipulated. In the past, news reporters had more expertise and analytical skills than todays reporters. The media were held to higher standards to report the truth. Today the added competition from cable networks and instant internet news sites have caused the media to scramble to report quickly and check facts later. It is all about getting a news exclusive. It is a frustrating reality for anyone who wishes to have accurate, verified information but is also a bold opportunity for the government to exploit.

The American government is masterful at using disinformation as a weapon. It may be introduced through public announcements made by high ranking officials. It may surface through the discovery of funding for new projects in congressional budget reports; whether the funding is real or not. It may be uncovered in documents the become declassified. These documents can also be completely fabricated to make it appear America has a greater capability than they do, or deceive others from what is truly going on. Not all "leaks" are accidental, some are part of a disinformation campaign.

North Korea would have a difficult time understanding the leaking of sensitive information or having information being stolen and made public. They may understand the stealing and selling of someone else's information though. American's are used to this happening and used to the media gobbling it up quickly. Some of the

141

"leaks" are actually made by the government as a means to disseminate disinformation. The more the government protests the leak, the more likely it is to be believed by the media, the public and enemy nations. If the information has any information that is salacious or compromising to a government official, the more likely it is to be believed. Given the severe punishment for criticizing the government in North Korea, they would certainly assume the information is true. Although it is commonplace for American's to criticize public officials, dictatorial governments have a hard time understanding American public protest.

The media likes to call in scientific experts to lend credence to stories. Most Americans accept information from these experts over government officials and news reporters. Its important to keep in mind that these scientific experts rely on grants and government funding to conduct their work and a certain percentage are willing to speak the official government narrative in exchange for continued funding and notoriety.

A classic example of disinformation being used as a weapon occurred towards the end of the old war. The U.S. disclosed that it had a missile defense shield capable of eliminating the threat that Soviet missiles could hit the U.S. A huge budget (falsified) was allotted for the project. Scientists lined up to share various components of the project with the media. Everyone was talking about the new "Star Wars" weapons. While some of those components do exist today, in the 1980s' it was pure fantasy; a bluff. The USSR invested a fortune trying to duplicate, counter and circumvent an advanced American weapons system that simply did not exist. The USSR bankrupted itself, and in a socialist society, where everything is owned or run by the government, bankruptcy meant failure of every system at once.

Lack of Money/Inability to Resupply

North Korea is cash poor and has relied on trade with mostly pariah nations to keep its elite in power and military loyal. If war were to occur, North Korea would find itself with a decreased ability to resupply, and may be cut of entirely. The U.S. would certainly declare those that help the North to be enemies as well. Although the poor would be affected first, eventually the lack of fuel and food would impact even the elites. Constant U.S. bombing would cause infrastructure damage that could not be rebuilt without outside supplies. The war would devolve into an unprecedented humanitarian crisis.

North Korea is aware of its own vulnerabilities. It is counting on America deciding the fight is not worth the risk and backing down. This is not likely to happen but there are many alternative scenarios that could prevent an all-out ground war.

Price of Fighting and Not Fighting

The United States is powerful, a goliath compared to North Korea. The current standoff empowers North Korea to appear as a martyr to others in the world who feel oppressed by America. If the U.S. is to preemptively attack, it will need to be a war of total destruction on a scale never before seen. The images and narratives reported by the press will show America as an aggressive giant, crippling a weaker nation with overwhelming force. The United States will lose its status as a peacemaker and moral compass of the world. It will be feared by some and distrusted by others. Whatever decisions the U.S. makes will impact world opinion.

If the United States was to back down to North Korea without a demonstrable resolution to the current situation, it would be exposed as a paper tiger. Allies would question America's resolve to honor defense pacts and America would lose its status as the defender of the free-world. Pariah nations would intensify efforts to build nuclear weapons following North Korea's lead.

One way or another, whether overt war, covert war, or diplomacy, the situation must have a viable resolution.

Nuke Attack

America has the nuclear capability to destroy the world multiple times over. It is the only country to use nuclear weapons in battle. The United States decision to use nuclear weapons over 70 years ago is still criticized by people internally and externally.

While the use of nuclear weapons has not been ruled out, it is highly unlikely the U.S. would choose this

144

option. It would be hypocritical for the United States to use nuclear weapons to prevent another country from having the ability to do so. Given that North Korea borders both Russia and China, any nuclear launch at the North could be confused by these countries as an imminent attack on them, triggering a retaliated attack. Unless the North attacks the U.S. with a nuclear weapon, it is unlikely these weapons will be used.

Terrorism

There are thought to be hundreds of North Korean agents in the United States. These agents have been known to commit suicide if captured and as such it cannot be ruled out that they would engage in suicide attacks within the United States. It is highly likely that they would coordinate with other terrorist groups to attack a common enemy.

While American agents would stand out in North Korea either by ethnicity or dialect; America is a melting pot and people are used to hearing others speak in foreign languages and originating from every country in the world.

North Korean agents would not be easily singled out, at least not by the general population.

Escalation

There is a risk North Korea could attack Japan or South Korea to draw them into the war. There is also a risk North Korea could stage an attack in the border regions of Russia and China which they would attribute to America.

There is a risk China or Russia may intervene on their own if they feel their territory is threatened, the bloodshed in North Korea becomes too great, or the influx of refugees becomes more than they can handle. China would likely be reluctant since it owes its economic prosperity to ongoing relations with the United States. Russia, will likely find other places in the world to conquest rather than engage America directly.

Land Grabs in other Places

The United States has military operations throughout the world and should a war break out in North Korea, many of these other conflict regions will become secondary to U.S. interests. A void of American troops in a region may present an opportunity for belligerents to advance their military and political goals in that region This places the burden of regional protection upon others. Saudi Arabia understands that it will need to take greater responsibility to protect itself should the U.S. become engrossed in North Korea and that Iran will take any opportunity presented by the lack of U.S. presence to its advantage. In its defensive interest, Saudi Arabia has built an Arab coalition, engaged with Israeli officials and purchased nuclear weapons from Pakistan (without international outcry).

While there is great hype that Russia wants to invade the Ukraine, it is not in Russia's strategic interest to do so. It is important to them that the government in Ukraine is friendly toward Russia, but Russia is more secure with an independent Ukraine as a buffer between it and the rest of Europe. Russia is more concerned about continued influence over Syria, enhancing relations with Turkey and swaying them away from U.S. influence, and possibly increasing influence in Cuba, Venezuela, and other Latin American countries.

Ironically, the current economic upswing in the United States is mainly built upon the increase in weapon sales to countries fearing attack in Europe, Asia, and the Middle East. The fear of war has had very positive impact on the U.S. economy.

Mass Production of Nukes

Once a country has the technology to build a nuclear bomb, they can build a hundred or a thousand. It is the initial one that presents a challenge. The mission thus becomes removing the current nuclear weapons in North Korea as well as destroying the ability to build more.

If North Korea builds more, it will become a threat not only to the United States but to all countries of the world (including China and Russia). It will be able to extort its way into the international community via threats. They may also become prosperous by selling the weapons to other rogue nations.

Collapse of Regime, Loose Nukes

China most fears a collapse of the North Korean regime. They prefer the known danger to an unknown replacement and the chaos that occurs during the transition period. As it stands, only Kim Jong Un can order the launch of a nuclear missile, but if something happens to him, there would be a power vacuum that could place control of the weapons in the hands of a dozen of people.

The United States does not fear such a collapse, as then North Korea problem would become China's worry.

Other Options

America has many options other than a full-scale attack on the North. Some of the alternatives come with a series of consequences. Some of the options removes the U.S. from the battlefield altogether.

China Attacks North Korea

(a) China wishes to become the premiere power and influence in the region. The United States could agree to support China's goal if it takes care of the North Korean problem.

(b) China is in the best position to attack North Korea and quickly secure the strategic weapons located on its border. North Korea is preoccupied with a U.S. attack. They would never suspect a sneak attack from China.

(c) China could also covertly attack North Korea by pretending to bring in Chinese troops to protect the North from a U.S. attack and then once in place, seize control. It is important to note that there have been some highly unusual meetings between Chinese and American top military brass, including General Dunford's visit to Chinese soldiers stationed on the border of North Korea.

Arm South Korea and Japan with Nukes

America could balance the playing field by giving nuclear weapons to Japan and South Korea. North Korea would then find itself in the same conundrum that all nuclear powers have, mutually assured destruction if the weapon is used.

Russia and China would find this arrangement unacceptable.

EMP Attack

Unlike the much-discussed possibility that North Korea could detonate a nuclear explosion high in the atmosphere to create an electro-magnetic pulse weapon (EMP), the U.S. already has a genuine EMP weapon. If used on North Korea it could disable computers, electronics, electric power, vehicles, guidance systems, and basically shut the North off from technology of any kind.

Such an attack would also impact parts of China, Russia, South Korea, and Japan. It would also impact airplanes and ships operating in the area.

Internet

America demonstrated its ability to shut down North Korean internet. It has greater tools available to conduct cyber-warfare. Most people are familiar with the world wide web (www) but few have encountered www2, www3, www4 etc., but they exist. Each is a mirror to the original world wide web backing up information in case something happens to the original.

The United States could surreptitiously replace the North Korean internet with a mirror version that appears to be the original but is actually controlled by the CIA. It would allow the U.S. to learn how the North conducts cyber-attacks but more importantly could be used to convince North Korea that they are making successful attacks when in fact everything they witness would only be occurring in an alternate reality. This system could also be used to make it appear America had infiltrated their systems.

150

At very least, this action would distract hackers from doing actual harm.

Assassination

Kim Jong Un has stated that he has survived several assassination attempts by the United States, which is possible. He should not be the primary target of an attack though. In order to neutralize the weapon development programs, it is the scientists that should be primary targets, as Israel targeted scientists in Iran.

Propaganda

North Korea keeps its population in control by limiting their information. Its leaders fear the population learning more about the outside world. As with propaganda campaigns from South Korea the U.S. could engage in balloon launches and provide small radios with access to stations broadcasting from Japan and American ships.

Whether true propaganda or simply true broadcasts which expose the North Korean propaganda, any ability to enlighten the population enhances the threat that the population can overthrow the government on is own.

Reunification

Both the North and the South want reunification. The leaders of the North, however, also fear reunification because many of their leaders would likely face trial for human rights violations. Kim Jong Un would also need to cede power to a South Korean leader.

A reunification deal could include provisions that the new government will pardon North Korean officials from prosecution. Kim Jong Un would still need to step down but he could be enticed by being hailed as the great leader who brought the two nations together, thus sealing a legacy comparable to his predecessors. He could also be provided with a life of luxury for the remainder of his days. Securing his legacy may be an acceptable motivation for him to abdicate.

Reintegration into World

While North Korea states it will never give up its nuclear weapons, perhaps the government would reconsider if North Korea could become part of the global community. North Korea is isolated, but not entirely by choice. The North wants a chance to be as successful as other nations, but efforts have been thwarted by the global community shunning the North.

If the North were allowed, they could become prosperous and successful. Over a long period of time the people and the regime itself would change and assimilate. Kim Jong Un could remain in power, and secure a legacy as the recreator of the modern North Korea. When China became more integrated with the world, especially its free trade with the United States and the reintegration of Hong Kong, it changed from a purely communist state to a blend of communism and capitalism. Exposure and connection with the outside world changed nearly every aspect of life in China. It is possible that North Korea would change as well if it became more integrated with the world.

China and Russia feeling threatened

China, Russia, and the United States have cooperated on sharing information about potential terrorist attacks. Terrorism is a major internal concern for all three countries.

China had 106 terrorist attacks/attempted attacks in the past 10 years which resulted in nearly 1000 deaths. The main perpetrators are Uyghur terrorists who mostly reside in the far western region of China near the border with Pakistan.

Russia had 1260 terrorist attacks/attempted attacks in the past 10 years which resulted in over 1200 deaths. The main perpetrators of terrorism in Russia are Chechen.

If evidence presents itself that North Korea is conspiring with either of these terrorist groups, or there is a risk that they have purchased or intercepted technology that originated in North Korea, China or Russia would take it upon themselves to invade. Neither country would hesitate the way the United States is currently doing, nor would they worry about world opinion. If either of these terrorist groups were found to be connected to North Korea, the risk of not doing anything would be too great for Russia or China to intervene.

Here is always a possibility, that such information may be planted by the United States as part of a disinformation campaign.

Conclusion

The situation in North Korea is very complex and involves others besides North Korea and the United States. Any action taken or not taken will impact the world as a whole.

May God help us all.

Bibliography

Albert, Eleanor. "Understanding the China-North Korea Relationship." Council on Foreign Relations, Council on Foreign Relations, 2017

Bajoria, Jayshree. "North Korea-Iran Nuclear Cooperation." Council on Foreign Relations, Council on Foreign Relations, 2010

Blomquist, Rachel, and Daniel Wertz. "An Overview of North Korea-Japan Relations." NCNK, 17 May 2017

Daniels, Jeff. "North Korea's Hidden Submarine Threat as Regime Warns 'Ready' for War." CNBC, CNBC, 17 Apr. 2017

"History of North Korea." Liberty in North Korea, 2017

Kelly, Robert E. "North Korea - South Korea Relations." North Korea - South Korea Relations - Al Jazeera Center for Studies, Al Jazeera, 2013

Nakashima, Ellen, and Philip Rucker. "U.S. Declares North Korea Carried out Massive WannaCry Cyberattack." The Washington Post, WP Company, 19 Dec. 2017

North Korea News. "Why North Korea Hates the U.S. and Vietnam Doesn't." NK News - North Korea News, 22 Sept. 2014

Pennington, Matthew. "The US and China Hold Quiet Military Talks amid North Korea Tensions." Business Insider, Business Insider, 30 Nov. 2017

Ramani, Samuel. "The Long History of the Pakistan-North Korea Nexus." The Diplomat, The Diplomat, 31 Aug. 2016

Ramani, Samuel. "The North Korea-Cuba Connection." The Diplomat, The Diplomat, 7 June 2016

Rinna, Anthony. "North Korea-Russia Relations: Limitations Behind the Façade of Friendship." IAPS Dialogue: The Online Magazine of the Institute of Asia & Pacific Studies, 10 Apr. 2017

Robinson, Julian. "Is Kim Jong-Un Planning to Use Submarines to Launch Nuclear Attack? How 50 North Korean Subs 'Went Missing' Sparking Panic in Seoul and Tokyo." Daily Mail Online, Associated Newspapers, 13 Apr. 2017

Additional books by Dr. John Bridges available on Amazon

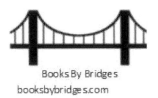

Books By Bridges
booksbybridges.com

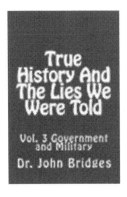

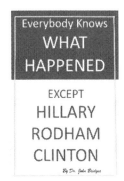

BOOKSBYBRIDGES.COM

Made in the USA
San Bernardino, CA
24 February 2018